REASON
TO
BELIEVE

A PERSONAL STORY BY RON TESORIERO

Published by Ron Tesoriero
Box 1032 Post Office
Gosford New South Wales
Australia 2250

Website: www.reasontobelieve.com.au

ISBN 978-0-646-47433-5

KDR Design+Print 61-2-4365 4010

CHAPTERS

1   THE LAWYER, THE BUSINESSMAN AND THE PRIEST 1

2   THREE CHILDREN AND A HUNDRED
    THOUSAND WITNESSES 15

3   A DEAL'S A DEAL 23

4   THE SCIENTIST 29

5   THE SECRETARY 51

6   THE STIGMATIST 61

7   THE TELEVISION CELEBRITY 65

8   THE GOOD THIEF 69

9   PERFUME AND BLOOD 73

10 MY MOTHER 77

11 SIGNS FROM GOD. 81

12 THE HEART THAT SUFFERS 89

13 THE REAL PRESENCE 99

14 CENTURIES OF STORIES. 105

15 MY MOTHER AND OUR MOTHER 111

16 POST MORTEM 117

17 BLIND MEN SEE 125

18 THE HEART OF THE MATTER 137

19 LOVE'S SECOND NAME 145

20 SCIENCE AND AN OLD EVANGELISATION . . . , ... 155

21 SCIENCE AND A NEW EVANGELISATION 167

22 FAITH OF MY FATHERS 185

PREFACE

This book is one man's gift of truth.

From the almost forgotten, God-given phenomenon of Fatima, to scientific evidence that the flesh and blood of Jesus is truly in the Eucharist, this work of Ron Tesoriero is based on fact.

But despite his constant worldwide search for proof of the teachings that the Gospels have offered for 2000 years, it was in his home town of Sydney where he was personally touched by the existence of Jesus in our lives; it was through the death of his mother. It is difficult to imagine anyone who reads this chapter with an open mind not being moved.

Ron also tells the story of a meeting in Adelaide where we were launching a film we had made on the Eucharist. After showing the film an elderly blind man stood and declared that he had seen the film from start to finish.

He documents the story and the intense testing of a mystic from Bolivia named Katya Rivas.

Ron's book gives Reason to Believe in a God of Love and Mercy; a God who exists, hears our prayers and even intervenes in our lives... and who now waits for the love of His Children.

Michael Willesee

CHAPTER 1

THE LAWYER, THE BUSINESSMAN AND THE PRIEST

"Someone needs you."

"I'm pretty busy. Does he have an appointment?" I murmured while continuing to scrutinize the document before me. I didn't look up at the woman peering around the slightly open door.

"No," she said.

"Well tell him to make one." Still I didn't look up.

"Your next client is due in an hour." She managed to make a statement of fact into a plea which in itself was unusual, her being so unassuming and efficient. She'd been my assistant for a long time, almost from the first days of setting up my legal practice thirty years ago, so I had only to sigh and look up to convey my displeasure at the prospect of being interrupted.

She waited. In my lack of response she read my capitulation and said, "I'll tell him you only have a few minutes."

Tesoriero, Henderson and Cotter was a successful legal practice in Gosford, a small waterfront town about an hour north of Sydney. Clients always made appointments. That this one ignored the accepted protocol was curious in itself. I put my work aside. She smiled and gently closed the door. When it opened again, a small smiling man in his late fifties came in. He wore a heavy black serge cassock reaching to the floor and a white collar drawn like a bandage separating his head from the mountain of black below. In Australia in 1987 one hardly saw men wearing their faith on their sleeves anymore and so the stranger seemed more like a character from an Italian film than a real person. He looked quite literally as if he came in from another world, a world I had left behind when I finished school many years ago. He was unmistakably a Catholic priest. My days as a Catholic schoolboy, although remote and although I no longer practised my faith, had left in me, if not belief, then indelible vestiges of social decorum. I was indifferent to what these men preached but this didn't preclude the respect, albeit somewhat patronising, even juvenile, which was their due.

"Good morning, Father," I said and rose to greet him.
"Ron Tesoriero? How do you do. My name is Father William Aliprandi. I've recently been appointed the parish priest of Kincumber."
I knew Kincumber, a nearby village at the foot of Kincumber mountain which was hardly a mountain but was the highest point in the Central Coast region overlooking meandering inland estuaries and the blue strip of Pacific ocean along Australia's eastern border.
"My boss," he continued adjusting his spectacles, "the Bishop of Broken Bay, has instructed me to build a church and a school for the parish. But the parish is a poor one, and has no land; mostly young working class families, tradesmen; a couple of fellas work in the quarry. As for myself, I, er, well, I have no money either." He smiled unapologetically. At this point, I leant back in my chair and awaited the inevitable next step in the interchange which, in one way or another, would be a hand stretched out for a donation.
"Well how can I help you Father?"
"I've found it," he announced triumphantly and very pleased.
"You've found the money?"
"Not the money, I've found the land. I walk past it every day and it's the right land. At the moment it doesn't look like much; thick bush, and there's only a small dirt track on the one side. But once it's

cleared it'll be ideal because it's near the village."

"Is it for sale?"

"No."

"Do you know who owns it?"

"No, but I..."

"So, let me get this straight. You don't have any money whatsoever. You want to buy some land which is not for sale."

"That's correct. But there's more." Father Aliprandi continued unfazed by my tone. "You see every day I've been praying about this business of building a church and then I felt strongly that this was the right place for it, and so I walked on it and I made a cross with some stones and now every day I go there and I kneel on the ground and I pray to God that we might obtain it."

Nothing in all my years in the legal profession had prepared me for the priest's naiveté and the astonishingly calm confidence with which he proclaimed his superstitions. I, quite unusually, had absolutely nothing to say. Father Aliprandi though, was on a roll.

"I have some help though. I've enlisted some help from a woman who is, I hope, influential."

"Good. You seem to surely need the help of someone." I said, "Who is she?"

"Was," Father Aliprandi corrected me with a chuckle. "Your question should be 'Who was she? She's not quite with us, er, so to speak. Been dead some seventy years or more. 1909 I think she died."

I stiffened. My hands, folded complacently in calculated professional composure, came apart. I reached for my pen and began fidgeting with it while I gathered every last ounce of civility for my rejoinder. I surprised myself with my polite banality.

"Dead?"

"Well yes, although I prefer to think of her as having passed on. Being dead is such a horribly final thing, don't you think? Yes. Well er…her name is Mary MacKillop. She was a nun, the founder of an order of teaching nuns in Australia, the Sisters of St Joseph of the

Father Aliprandi on the land where he prayed

Sacred Heart, and the best bet Australia has for one day having its very own backyard saint. Exceptional she was. Tough as nails. She founded the old orphanage down in South Kincumber on the water's edge, next to the old church, the second oldest in Australia I'm told. 1842. Anyway we're hoping the Holy Father will beatify her soon. But I'm rambling on, aren't I?"

The weight of my non-response launched the priest on to the point of his history lesson.

"All I've done is nail a relic of hers to a tree on that land, and I'm praying for her intercession, so we can have it."

"A relic?" I was casting back into my past for a definition. The cheerful gullibility of the man left me quite dazed.

"Oh it's not much. Just a small snippet of one of the habits she used to wear."

This conversation did not sit comfortably with what I was used to. In my world reality was neatly framed in established land conveyancing procedures and so, in a gesture of resolution, of returning to earth, I swept the nonsense away with a large map rolled into a baton which I brandished like a sword in front of the little priest.

"Let's have a look then, shall we?" I said in my getting down to business voice. "This is a Gosford Council Zoning map and you should be able to locate the land in question. So have a look and see if you can show me where it is?"

The priest rose so as to take in the scale of the diagram which covered the whole desk and fell with rolled edges down the side. Without any trouble Father Aliprandi pointed out a two centimeter square, coloured orange and outlined in black.

"This it? You're sure?" I asked.

"That's the one. Maps make the world look so small and manageable, don't they?" mumbled the priest, and sat back.

I scrutinized it, clearly decoding the fine text, and what I read brought me relief.

"Father, I'm sorry to disappoint you but you'll never be able to build your church on this particular piece of property. City council regulations have it zoned as reserved for conservation and you're simply not allowed to build a church or a school on it."

The victory for the real world and its august regulations, unshakeable by priests or their gods, their saints or their prayers, was not quite so delectable as I had anticipated. The priest simply stayed silent and dropped his gaze. An unfamiliar sensation of pity then moved me to say, as I rose to farewell Father Aliprandi, " Let me see what I can do. I'll make some enquiries and investigate other appropriately zoned property in the area. If you just leave your details with my secretary, I'll let you know the results. It will take a couple of weeks."

"Thank you kindly, young man, and may the good Lord bless you."

We said farewell and somewhat bemused at his naiveté I thought no more about the unusual encounter.

A few days later another stranger was in my office. He was a businessman and he had made an appointment. He came straight to the point.

"I need to liquidate my company as soon as possible. In fact really quickly, before the end of the financial year. There will be some ...er ... significant financial advantages for me when this transpires. To do this I have to sell a piece of land in Terrigal. It shouldn't be too much of a problem. It's in a pretty good location. I already have someone who is interested in buying it."

"Well it all seems pretty straightforward then," I said.

"Not exactly. My big problem is getting rid of a second piece of land and I was hoping that whoever buys the Terrigal land could be induced to buy it. It's not worth much, so I'd be more than happy to let it go for a song, as long as the deal can be closed very quickly."

"What's the problem with it?" I asked.

"Problems," he countered, " more than one. You see its biggest problem is that there's no infrastructure servicing it; no decent roads, in fact difficult to access, no water, electricity, all that sort of stuff." Again I pulled out my zoning map. He pointed to the second piece of land. I slumped back in my chair and sighed very deeply, which must have made him think his problem was a very big one indeed. "That bad?" he murmured.

"No, no… it's just … no, it's nothing." I stared at the map, and then out the window.

"Wait a minute," the businessman stood up and bent forward to examine the map. "Could I just check something?" he asked and took the map, found what he was searching for and declared, "I thought so. It's not current, this map. It's not the most recent one. The newest zoning regulations have proclaimed my land as residential. So that's good news surely. Much less restrictive."

I knew what he was saying was significant but his words had slid into the background, almost as if he was in a movie and the sound had been switched off. I tried really hard to bring myself back into the situation but all I kept thinking was that somewhere on his land was a tree with a scrap of a dead nun's clothing nailed to it.

Friday would be an unforgettable day. The businessman and I were in my office to meet the prospective buyer for the Terrigal land. He had agreed to the purchase price and had driven up from Sydney with his attorney to close the deal. It seemed an amicable enough arrangement, purely procedural, and I was looking forward to an early lunch. But then, without prior warning or consultation, my client suddenly pulled the rug out from under all of us with a huge and unexpected about-turn.

"I've done some thinking and I've changed my mind. It's too cheap. I want two hundred thousand more."

"But we agreed. Over the phone. We had a deal." The buyer was outraged.

"I know," said my client smoothly, "but I haven't signed a thing and

I've changed my mind."

"Two hundred thousand dollars! That's a helluva lot more than I agreed to over the phone. This is ridiculous. I've been in this business for thirty five years and I've never had to deal with anything of this kind."

The atmosphere in my office became predictably hostile as one man's indignation clashed with the other's refusal to budge. I was unprepared for this new demand and felt squeezed between anger at being so unprofessionally compromised and a vague apprehension that there was a lot to lose. In the heat of the wrangling I had to do something to save the negotiations from collapse. Quick lateral thinking was summoned. I found a gap in the verbal combat.

"The Terrigal land is zoned part residential and part conservation, right? The council regulations permit a certain discretionary planning elasticity regarding development on the conservation land if that land shares similar characteristics with the adjacent residential land to be developed. As long as environmental factors are not infringed, and as long as they can see the congruence of vegetation type etcetera, they allow some encroachment." Three angry men glared at me.

"What this means for you," I concluded looking at the disgruntled purchaser, " is that you get some extra allotments of land and some fabulous sea views as a bonus."

The purchaser and his attorney looked at each other and suspiciously at me.

"No. No, the deal's off," the Sydney buyer pronounced. He glared blackly at my client and left my office. Grabbing up his paperwork, his attorney followed. If he had had a free hand he would've slammed the door.

It was noon and we broke for lunch. I took the businessman to a restaurant nearby. There was someone I wanted him to meet. Father Aliprandi was already seated and I noted the effect his unusual attire had on the businessman. I brought the matter to a head.

"Father Aliprandi is keenly interested in the purchase of the Kincumber land to build a church and a school." I ventured.

"That suits me," said the businessman, "because I am all set to sell as soon as possible."

"Well now," said the priest, "Slow down a bit. I'm not the man with the cheque book. The Bishop still has to approve the purchase and then we'll have to start raising money. It may be a while yet."

Twenty minutes ago the businessman had shocked me with an extravagant demand for one piece of land and now he shocked me by veering in completely the opposite direction.

"I'll give it to you for $210 000 Ron will bear me out when I say it's a fraction of its market value. A steal."

"Well bargain or not, I still don't have the money or the permission right now, but I'm certain my superiors will be most interested. We need a little time."

"It's time that I can't afford," said the businessman, and grimaced, adjusted his serviette and then announced with deliberation, "Look here, I'll sell you an option on the land for a dollar."

"A dollar!" The priest was astonished

"That's right. You heard me. A dollar. And then when you get the rest of the money we'll settle."

Father Aliprandi broke out into hearty laughter. "Well now, let me see." He fumbled in his pockets and drew out odd coins. "Eighty cents. I owe you twenty."

"Done!"

We all laughed. The two men shook hands on the deal and Father Aliprandi said something which was to touch the seller more deeply than I could possibly imagine.

"For such an act of commitment to God, don't be surprised if you're blessed by God and good things happen to you, Even today."

The businessman and I were back in my office after lunch, reworking the contract of sale to include the new and higher sale price when the Sydney team unexpectedly returned.

"You're right," said the attorney, "about the encroachment possibility, and those extra allotments and those sea views. Pretty obscure clause you found in the legislation though. We've spent the last hour at the council office with the planning officer. It all seems in order and my client has agreed to the additional amount."

It was a huge sum of money initially and was now inflated by even more. The buyer kept silent throughout the rest of the negotiations. At the end though he sighed and said, "Where do I sign?"

With a massive workload I was back in the office early on Monday morning. The phone rang. I let it. I was too busy and none of the staff was in yet. Shrill and demanding it continued. I glared at it. It took no notice. I relented.

"Hallo."

The caller was too excited to notice my ill humour. It was the businessman.

"Ron, it's absolutely unbelievable!" He was exultant.

"What is?" I offered flatly.

"You haven't heard. Obviously you haven't heard. The market's crashed! All over the world."

"The stock market?"

"Of course," he said gleefully. "Which means that I would never be able to get the same price for my land today as I got last Friday. It's like winning the lottery. How lucky is that!"

"Luck?" I offered, thinking of the priest, thinking of the markets collapse. It was 11 October 1987, a day to which very, very few would attach the word 'luck', and luck seemed to be too fickle and mild to be involved with the fascinating sequence of events unravelling before my very curious eyes.

Some months passed while Father Aliprandi continued trying to raise the outstanding money. He wasn't even close to his target when another unforeseen purchase of land took place. This time the land in question was directly adjacent to the 'Aliprandi' land. And this time the purchaser was the government itself. A new high school was planned and so state-of-the-art new roads, water and electricity infrastructure were laid. Although this should have been extraordinarily fortunate for the priest's plans I started worrying that if he didn't hurry up and pay the outstanding balance, $210 000 minus one dollar, the businessman would prefer the extra million dollars he would now certainly get for the land to keeping his promise, which, after all, was only a verbal agreement. I offered to lend the priest the money just to help him secure it at the agreed, but now insanely low price.

There was a small hurdle though. In fact it was a thousand kilometre hurdle because the businessman had moved to the Gold Coast and I had nothing on paper to hold him to his word. Handshakes don't hold up too well in court. Speaking to him face to face seemed the best way to proceed. But where was I to find the time to fly to another city? What I saw on my desk the next day made me shake my head in disbelief: an airline ticket to that very same city to attend to totally unrelated business. The client who provided the ticket however would in years to come become integral and indispensable to my work and so I use the word 'unrelated' because that is how it seemed to me at the time.

I flew out, completed the work at hand and then set about connecting with the businessman to conclude the 'Aliprandi' land affair. I rang his number. Both of us were free at the time and agreed to meet. He gave me his address but, being in a strange city, I hadn't a clue where or how far away he was.

"Where are you right now, Ron?" he asked, and I gave him the address of the architectural firm where I had represented my client.

"It's probably easier if I just meet you there. Is that alright?"

The foyer was fashionably decorated with armchairs and glass tables and it was as good a place as any for a meeting, so I agreed. I found a comfortable chair and a newspaper and settled down to wait. No sooner had I read the headlines than the businessman walked in. He lived only a few blocks away. With him was an expensively dressed woman who might have been elegant were it not for the grim expression on her polished face which soured the whole effect.

"This whole thing is ridiculous. Absolutely insane," she protested.

"Honey, we've talked about this," he said to pacify her.

And to me she addressed her statement although it was clearly not to me she was talking. "The government has laid beautiful new roads and electricity and everything. It's worth twenty or thirty times as much now. We have absolutely no reason to accept this ridiculous amount."

"Let's not go there again," said her husband.

"We are perfectly entitled to. We are completely within the law to sell for its true value. Is that not so, Mr Tesoriero?"

"We have an agreement," I offered.

"Not on paper; no signatures; not in the eyes of the law. I'm not signing anything."

I was floundering. I didn't want to be the umpire in this domestic clash. I didn't want to alienate the businessman by standing up to his wife. I didn't want to disappoint the priest. The businessman looked straight at me and asked for the document to sign. Then, without a word, he instructed his wife to co-sign by giving her the pen and glaring at her in a way that must have carried the weight of a final verdict in their private married world. She did. We stood to shake hands.

"I gave my word to that priest. I want to honour it."

To my immense surprise he had refused to buckle to her arguments. He could have got away legally with reneging on his promises but he stayed true. The documents were signed and exchanged. I remember the relief. It was all over. Not for the first time was I completely wrong. It was anything but over.

The whole affair was remarkable, virtually unbelievable. Back home, later, I took my incredulity straight to Father Aliprandi.

"Did you really believe, when you first knelt down and prayed to obtain that particular piece of land, that it would all happen?"

"I had no doubt."

"How could you feel so certain?"

"It wasn't for me. I didn't personally want it. God did. For us. The people of Kincumber needed a church where they could honour and worship God. And their children needed a school where they could learn about him. God would not allow such plans for our benefit to be frustrated by lack of money. The God who created this world has not lost his power you know. I've set aside my life to work for him and I asked him for his help." Then he smiled and concluded, "I would have been surprised if he had not helped me."

Miracles to some are simple, I thought. Belief is hard.

God dealt in real estate? He stepped into the real here-and-now affairs of men? Even business affairs? Or was this just a freak series of convoluted co-incidences? I mean every day someone gets lucky and someone else loses out. That's just life. Or is it? Father Aliprandi had his land for a fraction of its market value, land with great infrastructure thrown in for nothing, and I had a major philosophical conundrum to deal with. What I had been privy to, no, more than that, actually involved in, was nothing short of extraordinary. Someone had prayed for the impossible and despite all odds, and in the most unorthodox way, it was granted. I even started thinking that my contribution was somehow deliberately orchestrated in the events which played themselves out in front of me. I was in something I didn't understand.

I told other people about it all and their reactions fell into basically two camps. Some said that it was all just co-incidence and that co-incidence happens all the time. Others said that this was unquestionably the hand of God at work. And I continued to puzzle over the differences. What is coincidence? What is an intervention by God? Does God intervene in the affairs of men?

CHAPTER 2

THREE CHILDREN AND A HUNDRED THOUSAND WITNESSES

Although I was raised as a Catholic, I, along with the vast majority of Catholics in the West, had ceased to practise my faith as a young adult. Together with my childhood I left my faith behind the school gates of St Joseph's College and ventured out to university and the 'real world'. My pre-occupation was with my career, my business, and eventually my family. I didn't need or have time for religion. I was doing fine without it. Very well in fact. But this whole 'Aliprandi' land incident opened a door through which I felt compelled to peer, to investigate a little further before I closed it with some satisfactory rational explanation. There was one. Of that I was sure.

And so it was that I began to explore other 'interventions' of God, beginning with something vaguely remembered from my schooldays, something about three Portuguese children and the Virgin Mary, something about a place called Fatima.

Armed with every book I could buy on the subject, I started investigating. In summary, this is what I found:

Just before the end of the First World War, on exactly the same day, 13 May 1917, two events took place simultaneously. On the extreme east of Europe two men were on a train destined for St Petersburg, the capital of Russia. Their names were Lenin and Trotsky. On the other western extreme of Europe, in Portugal, three illiterate peasant children claimed that the Virgin Mary had appeared to them and spoken to them. She told them things that had to do with the rise of communism, the coming of another, even worse world war, the future of humanity, and more significantly, what could be done to avert the dire forecast. The children were concerned that they wouldn't be believed and so the Lady promised them that on 13 October 1917 at noon a public miracle would validate the truth of her appearances and revelations.

At the predicted time and place people gathered in their thousands. Dr Jose Garrett, a professor from the Faculty of Sciences at the University of Coimbra, enjoyed a commanding view of the crowd of people gathered at the Cova d'Iria. With his powerful binoculars, he calculated a figure in excess of 100 000 people. The local newspapers reported only 70 000. It was bitterly cold and steady driving rain had fallen all day. Everything and everyone in the crowd was drenched and muddy. Twelve o'clock came and went. Nothing happened. Then at solar noon, noon according to the whole planet and not noon according to the local Portuguese, the great mass of clouds parted like a thick curtain to reveal the sun directly behind it. Lucia, one of the three children looked up and shouted, "She's coming!"

Many thousands of witnesses corroborated the events which followed in the next twelve minutes. The sun, or what was thought to be the sun, moved from place to place. Some said it 'danced', throwing out beautiful multi-coloured lights like a spinning colour wheel, which played across the rapt expressions in the rolling landscape. Faces, bodies, trees, umbrellas, rocks and grass all reflected brilliant and changing colours. Then it spun on its axis. Its rim became scarlet and it scattered bursts of flame across the sky.

The entire sun began to plummet to earth. Beauty turned to terror. It zigzagged from side to side. Thousands cried out in fright. Many fell to their knees and prayed. At a critical moment it stopped. Then for a few seconds a strange wind blew through the area and everyone's sodden clothes instantaneously dried as did the muddy ground and all the puddles. Witnesses declared that all of a sudden they were dry and felt comfortable and clean. A 100 000 people present and everyone within a twenty mile radius saw a startling celestial event never experienced before. Many thought it was the end of the world.

Did the Virgin Mary really appear and speak to the children? Did the strange and terrifying movements of the sun actually happen, and if they did, was it a co-incidence that they happened at the exact time and place predicted by three little children? Or did 100 000 people become so emotionally involved that they fell victim to an hypnotic mass hysteria which made them all believe they saw something which in fact did not happen? My mind was buzzing with questions and curiosity and so I turned to accounts given by witnesses present on the day. One after another, young and old, believers and atheists, educated and illiterate, peasants and city dwellers, soldiers and priests, all gave virtually the same account. An unprecedented, inexplicable event of cosmic proportions had without doubt occurred.

Of most interest to me were those corroborating statements given not by the pious and devoted believers, but by those sent expressly to perform their duties: journalists, government officials and police officers. Portugal was at the time a Socialist regime with a strongly anti-Catholic agenda. The press was encouraged to cultivate atheistic world views which it was suggested would bring Portugal into the modern world, out of the 'dark ages of oppression by the Church.' The two major newspapers were in the stable of the reigning political powers. For weeks both had been adamantly attacking the purported

The Three children of Fatima

Part of the crowd observing the miracle of the Sun [1917]

Pope visits Fatima [2000]. In the crown of the statue of the Virgin Mary is the bullet taken from the Holy Father after the assassination attempt of 1981

supernatural sightings as fraudulent and were committed to exposing the whole drama as hysterical provincial superstition. Weeks of mockery changed overnight. Both editors carried corroborative headlines declaring a miracle beyond all cosmic laws had carried them back to biblical times. We were all, they said, weeping and praying.

Just as fascinating were reports given by people who lived nearby but who consciously avoided going to the predicted place because they thought the whole thing was sheer nonsense. All these so-called objective, unemotional, unconnected observers confirm in every detail what was reported by the crowd. The co-incidence theory was slowly but surely losing its power of conviction.

I learned that the Catholic Church has a particular way of looking at miracles. It sees miracles as an intervention of God in the natural world. The laws of that world, as we, and as science knows them, are suspended. The New Catholic Encyclopedia notes that a miracle has three characteristics: 1. It must be extraordinary. 2. It must be perceptible to the senses. 3. It must be produced by God in a religious context as evidence of his presence. Miracles do not issue from man but they do relate to human life. The Church sees in authenticated miracles, visions, or paranormal signs, a kind of continuous presence of God with his people, an intervention not occasioned by our merits but due solely to God's initiative, mercy and love for his creatures, especially man. A true Christian believes in miracles simply because Jesus himself performed them two thousand years ago. Then they were for the benefit of the people of Palestine so that they would believe in what He said and who He claimed to be. The same goes for us today. Miracles seem to be invitations to faith.

The process of the approval of miracles is not simple. It involves the combined work of doctors, theologians, technical experts in various scientific fields, and often years of research before the Church will approve or not approve a claim. And so, only in the 1930's, after lengthy investigation, did the Catholic Church deem the events at Fatima worthy of belief. Yet at the same time there seemed to be little official endorsement of the message of Fatima which might have helped people, like myself, in their discernment of the phenomenon and the significance of the message.

Essentially the message of the Fatima revelation is a peace plan for our times. You can imagine then, that I was really surprised that it was of little interest in the secular world, and scarcely more in the Catholic press. War is a result of humanity's sin, the Virgin Mary said, and can be averted by a return to God, by prayer and sacrifice. Surely something like this should have been front page news: God's own Peace Plan! Yet many priests I questioned were uninterested and the common response was that what happened at Fatima was a private revelation, not part of the deposit of faith, and therefore no Catholic was bound to believe it. But, I argued, why then do Catholics praying the Creed at Mass acknowledge that, 'God has spoken through the prophets,' and why would he not speak through his prophets today, especially if the message communicated was about creating world peace? With such weighty matters are we entitled to dismiss a message under the label of 'private revelation'? My question was answered when I read what John Paul II said in 1982 at Fatima. He quoted the Second Vatican Council's position on private revelations:

'The Church has always taught and continues to proclaim that God's revelation was brought to completion in Jesus Christ, who is the fullness of that revelation, and that no new public revelation is to be expected before His glorious manifestation. If the Church has accepted the message of Fatima it is, above all, because the message contains a truth and a call whose basic content is the truth and call of the gospel itself. *'Repent and believe in the gospel.'* These are the first words that Jesus addressed to humanity. The message of Fatima is, in its nucleus, a call to conversion and repentance as in the Gospel.'

So clearly, what was happening on the ground, was not happening at the top. The Pope himself was acutely conscious of the meaning of the Fatima revelations, a consciousness magnified and publicised by a very personal trauma. The 13 May 1981 was the anniversary of the first Marian apparition at Fatima. On that day in Rome, at point blank range, he was shot in the chest. Miraculously he survived the assassination attempt, the bullet missing his vital organs by a hair's breadth. In his mind there was no doubt at all that his life had been spared by the 'intervention' of the Virgin Mary and on the 13th May, the very next year, he travelled to Fatima to thank her publicly. He brought with him the bullet that was removed from his body and it was mounted in a bejeweled crown worn by a statue of Our Lady of Fatima in a chapel built on the site of the apparitions.

"It is not only to express my gratitude to Our Lady that I am going on a pilgrimage to Fatima. I go to that blessed place to hear anew, in the name of the whole Church, the message which resounded 65 years ago on the lips of the Common Mother, concerned for the fate of her children. That message reveals itself to be more urgent today than ever."

In a later compilation of his personal reflections called 'Memory and Identity' he wrote:

"Could I forget that the event in St Peter's Square took place on the day and at the hour when the first appearance of the Mother of Christ to the poor little peasants has been remembered for over sixty years at Fatima in Portugal? For, in everything that happened to me on that very day, I felt that extraordinary motherly protection and care, which turned out to be stronger than a deadly bullet.

Around Christmas 1983 I visited my attacker in prison. We spoke at length. Ali Agca, as everyone knows, was a professional assassin. This means that the attack was not his own initiative; it was someone else's idea; someone else had commissioned him to carry it out. In the course of our conversation it became clear that Ali Agca was still wondering how the attempted assassination could possibly have failed. He had planned it meticulously, attending to every detail. And yet his intended victim had escaped death. How could this have happened?

The interesting thing was that his perplexity had led him to the religious question. He wanted to know about the secret of Fatima, and what the secret actually was. This was his principal concern; more than anything else he wanted to know this.

Perhaps those insistent questions showed that he had grasped something really important. Ali Agca had probably sensed that over and above his own power, over and above the power of shooting and killing, there was a higher power. He began to look for it. I hope and pray that he found it."

So significant was the message of Fatima in the mind of John Paul II that not only did he earn the popular name of 'The Fatima Pope' but on 13 October 2000, underlining the significance of what had happened on the 13 October so many years before, he dedicated the third millennium to Our Lady of Fatima.

CHAPTER 3

A DEAL'S
A DEAL

There were four of us in the room, three lawyers and a merchant banker, all successful and prosperous men in their prime, and all brothers. Collectively we represented the happy ending of the clichéd fairy tale. A struggling immigrant, our father, Antonino Tesoriero from Panarea, an island near Sicily, came to the 'lucky' country with a dollar in his pocket, worked hard, and made sacrifices to provide superior education for his sons, who then all rewarded him with lucrative achievements and fine reputations.

Vincent, at 46, the merchant banker, was the real star amongst us. He was the deputy general manager of one of Australia's biggest insurance companies. He earned a large salary and had acquired, besides degrees from Sydney University, an MBA, and a reputation for having studied at Harvard, an impressive collection of valuable properties and investments. The sum total of his remarkable success was brutally reduced and contained within the very object of our attention: Vince's black briefcase. It would have looked very official and appropriate in the right environment but here, in the whiteness of the room, it was quite out of place. Every document, diploma, title deed, and share certificate was pristinely kept and organised. Vince was a man who certainly had his affairs in order. But not his life. Cancer was voraciously consuming his pitiful body and in a week, we were told, he would be dead.

Even so, from his hospital bed he was meticulously ensuring that his last will and testament coincided with the contents of the briefcase and that his brothers were clear on its execution. Conscious use of his mental faculties was limited to a couple of days and he knew it, and was squeezing every last useful minute from the time remaining. He asked that I make sure his land taxes were paid on time. Then he reminded me again. Damn the land taxes, I thought. What difference is it going to make to you? Only a miracle could save him. Filled as I was with an agonising sense of foreboding, of loss and grief, and with a new dim awareness of the possibility of prayer and miracles, I did what millions have done before me: I made a deal with God.

"Save my brother Lord and I'll work for you for the rest of my life."

Not confident enough in my own ability to petition a God I had for so long ignored, I took inspiration from Father Aliprandi's real estate success and procured a relic of Mary MacKillop which my mother pinned on Vince's pyjamas. Vince did not improve and I knew I had to act. I managed to get hold of Father Aliprandi and he, without hesitation, travelled an inconvenient 70 km on a late night train to administer to my brother the last rites and hear his confession. We were now alone with Vince. He had made his peace with God and then he made his very last physical action. He lifted his head with great effort to receive Holy Communion. Within hours he lapsed into a coma and the day after that he was dead.

I scrutinised the black briefcase lying next to the body of my brother. In that moment I knew two things. I mean I 'knew' them in a significant way, a way that changed me. Firstly, I knew that my brother was not the lifeless corpse I could see. My brother, and by extension, myself and every one of us, is something more than the bodies we leave behind. Vince's body was lying there, but Vince was not. He was somewhere else. Secondly, I knew that wherever he was he didn't need his briefcase.

We were brought up as Christians, attended Christian schools and were citizens of a nominally Christian culture. To be a Christian means to believe in Jesus Christ and his promises that an eternal paradise awaits us after death if we follow his teaching in this brief and often difficult life. Yet that 'Christian' world we were immersed in was not convinced, it seemed, in its central belief. There was certainly little encouragement to be eligible for the greatest achievement of them all, a place in an eternal paradise, our true unimaginably perfect home. In fact, acquiring of the contents of that briefcase demanded an engagement with a world which dismisses, or at the very least, avoids belief in any thing other than itself. What was in that briefcase clamoured for undivided attention, even here at the very end. It seemed to me all of a sudden so irrational to regard it as relevant.

I mourned the drain on the limited time and energy of our lives spent in filling our briefcases with things which have to do only with enjoying this earthly life, a life which is but a grain of sand compared with all the sand on the shore of eternity. Deep inside me something shifted and I was filled with a profound conviction that I would spend whatever time was left to me in filling my 'briefcase' with things I could take with me.

"God didn't answer my prayer." I said to Father Aliprandi.
"Are you sure about that?" he asked.
"There's not any way to save him now. You prayed and asked God for help when you wanted the land for the church and school, and his answer was really impressive and I was a witness to it. So tell me Father," I challenged, "what did I do wrong? Did I say the wrong words or what?"
"You did nothing wrong. God always listens to every prayer. He told us didn't he, *'Ask and thou shalt receive.'*

"But I did and I didn't receive. I asked for my brother to be saved. And that never happened."

The priest was silent for a while and when he spoke it was with thoughtful conviction. "I think that when God does not give us exactly what we ask for it is because he wants to give us something even better. Your prayer was not ignored. God did not heal Vince miraculously as you wanted. He did something infinitely more significant. He was more good to you and to Vincent than you can even begin to imagine."

"You mean the last confession and communion?"

"Do you realise, Ron, what a grace it is to be able to put one's spiritual life in order with a good and valid confession, and to experience the peace and weightlessness that the sacrament brings before dying? And don't consider it any minor thing to receive the real and true Jesus in a state of grace just hours before the end. What a blessing! Do you for one moment think," Father Aliprandi asked in a very compelling soft voice, "that your being present, your seeing it for yourself was a coincidence? God not only saved Vincent for the next life, the eternal one, but he made sure you were there to confirm it. Now if that isn't such unimaginable kindness, I don't know what is?"

The wisdom of the priest penetrated clear and true to the kernel of my own equivocation. I was sad, terribly sad, and even disappointed that Vince was not alive, that God had not performed in the way I wanted him to. But I was not angry. Not in the way some bereaved people are. I've heard of those whose tragedies cause them to curse God and refuse to ever consider Him as anything but malevolent. Was I willing to believe that He had out-manoeuvred me in generosity? Was I able to experience some kind of consolation, even just the slightest sliver of joy at the outcome?

The bargain I made lay before me, clear and provocative, demanding engagement. Had I received even more than I asked for? And if so, what did that do to my side of the deal?

CHAPTER 4

THE
SCIENTIST

By 1993 I was on a new path. I had returned to the practice of the faith and was investigating other claims of divine intervention which were taking place around the world. I had taken time off from my legal work and bought myself a camera. Bill Steller, who had worked for years as a filmmaker for broadcast television, became my teacher and helped me learn the operating skills for recording sound and image. But even more important was his teaching me how to cover a scene comprehensively and then how to structure and assemble the footage by editing it all together.   Soon we were making documentaries of my research into claims of supernatural experiences, claims of extraordinary experiences attributed to the hand of God.

On one trip to a place called Conyers in the USA we met and filmed a fascinating man. He was very impressive; dedicated to his work, scrupulously thorough and courageously open-minded. He was a professor, born in Bolivia, who had lectured for many years in European universities as a neuropsychophysiologist. He was an expert in relating the physical and chemical activities of the brain to human behaviour. Some of his books are recommended texts in certain university departments in the Spanish speaking world where the brain and its activity are studied. He had been an outspoken atheist but after examining some baffling cases he was now less strident, although not entirely converted either. He was a warm, humble and likable man with a mellifluous cello undertone in his voice, one which wouldn't have sounded out of place on an opera stage. His name was Professor Ricardo Castanõn.

Around the world people were claiming to have supernatural and transcendental experiences of apparitions and revelations, and Professor Castanõn was challenging these claims, and so separating truth from fiction. To do this he sought to use the best science, medicine and psychiatry had to offer in theory and technology. The Catholic Church came to know of his work and, at times, called on him to conduct investigations on its behalf.

He would use state-of-the-art equipment to ascertain what was occurring in the auditory and visual centres of the brain when alleged mystics were seeing and hearing things which were non-existent to the rest of us. Activity from specific centres of the brain was registered as wavelengths on monitors attached to an electroencephalogram (EEG), a highly sensitive electronic apparatus. First a pattern of wavelengths for the person's normal active alert consciousness was established. Then the supposed mystic was instructed to pray or to meditate or to engage with their divine communicant in their chosen manner. He found that in some cases, when the person said that they were seeing or hearing Jesus, they would produce delta brain waves precisely at those moments. This extremely rare pattern of wave formation only occurs in specific instances: comatose patients, in exceptional cases of extremely deep sleep, and interestingly, also sometimes in suckling babies. A delta wave state is impossible to simulate or fake. It is also scientifically contradictory for a person to be alert, awake and communicating while registering delta waves. They were thus significant indicators of authenticity.

"Here we are," he said to me in his sonorous Spanish accent, "studying a woman who says she has visions of the Virgin Mary and Jesus Christ and thousands of Americans are believing her, yet no one is testing or researching the validity of her claims. Astonishing! Here in the United States you can study anything. Absolutely anything. There is virtually no restriction on scientific research." He chuckled and continued. "They have carried out studies to determine from what side of a bicycle a child is more likely to fall. But where are the scientists when this type of case comes up?"

"I suppose to be a good scientist you have to be skeptical and it seems that skepticism is what dissuades scientists from being interested in studying these cases," I offered.

"Yes. But there is a difference between being skeptical and being closed minded. I think we have to approach these matters with an open mind. Our mind is like a parachute. We can only expect that it will work when it is open. I am not a believer. But I am not closed to any debate or better still to some good solid science on the matter. How can any scientist call himself a scientist if he automatically dismisses any possibility? I investigate these mystics from many angles: psychologically, are they mentally stable, are they delusional, is it about the ego seeking publicity and attention? And in their lives are they simple, holy and humble or is greed for money a motivation?"

"So then you'd have to say that you're having problems as an atheist if you have scientific evidence pointing in the opposite direction."

"Well I've always considered myself completely rational. I believe in science."

"But now you're seeing results which your own science claims are impossible, like people fully awake and talking while registering Delta waves. "

"Yes, I would say that I, as a scientist , have no explanations…yet."

"And," I hesitated, "could it be that the only rational answer is to acknowledge some kind of divine hand at work?"

"I am a man; I live and then I die and it's all over. This is all I know right now."

Professor Castanõn and I then considered another case. This time two people were claiming to have mystical experiences of Jesus. They were placed in the same room and they each claimed to have a vision of Jesus at the same time, and for the same time. Each had been wired up with electrodes linked to monitors measuring brain activity while their clinical behaviour was being filmed. Both were active and alert. Yet both registered delta brain wave activity at the same time and for the same time. The results from the EEG appeared unique. Ricardo was intrigued.

"I have never seen anything like this," he muttered in disbelief.

In yet another investigation some months later another subject who had claimed to also have mystical experiences was given Holy Communion while being monitored and filmed. Her name was Patricia Talbot. She was from Ecuador. She turned to Ricardo and said, "The moment I received Communion I felt this extraordinary presence of Christ as if He was caressing my forehead."

Again the results of the EEG recordings were thoroughly perplexing. The subject was fully awake and physically active and yet at the very moment the communion wafer touched her tongue the monitor readings showed a delta wave state in her brain.

"What do you make of it?" I probed. He sighed. I pushed for a response.

"Could your test results be explained by some sort of psychic power, mind over matter, or the combined mental power of several people?" Shaking his head and in a quiet pensive way he concluded, "I do not think we can explain these things. We think that man is very intelligent and that we know everything. Sometimes we have to be humble and say, here is another kind of power that we do not understand. And that could be, I say 'could be', God.'"

Yet another case found us with a subject, Julia Kim, in South Korea. She reported having visions of Jesus and the Virgin Mary. A Korean neurologist was present and the question posed prior to the tests was a familiar one. Was it possible for a fully conscious human being to register delta brainwaves on the EEG? His reply was an emphatic and simple 'no.' The subject was asked to pray and the results showed unmistakable delta wave formations. Faced with mounting evidence Professor Ricardo Castanõn was becoming less sure of his strident atheism.

I had been back in Australia for a while when I came across a story in a newspaper which caught my attention. A statue of the Virgin Mary was weeping blood in Civitavecchia, near Rome. The headline read: 'A bloody miracle? No! Statues can't weep'. The journalist wrote about how a research chemist in an Italian University had been approached to explain how the Civitavecchia statue may be 'made' to weep. The reporter told how the chemist was able to replicate the effect by tampering with the statue. Whether or not the statue in question was tampered with we are not told. The text was grounded on a given assumption that some sort of hoax was involved. This assumption was automatically projected onto the literate public. No intelligent questions had been asked, questions I would have thought would have been standard procedure for an investigative journalist covering any story.

But I had questions: What were the circumstances in which it wept? Were there witnesses? Were they credible? Had the statue and whatever liquid was coming from it been subjected to scientific testing? Had the process been recorded on film?
The dilemma for the media in a case like this seems to be that the intellectual agenda has already been set by a pervasive contemporary philosophy which has decided that religion is for feeble and fearful minds, minds stuck in the past. The framework has been constructed and assumed to be one of alternatives; faith versus reason; science versus religion; today versus yesterday. To go so far as to even pursue a story such as this with anything other than a smirk on your face would be to entertain the possibility of something so outrageous that

the foundations of almost everything believed might be shaken. For the hardcore modern rationalists stories of the paranormal are titillating confections when applied to the past, to the gullible, to the superstitious, or to the under-developed world. They become decidedly embarrassing if found in their own 'civilised' backyard.

I could sense myself becoming irritated by the lack of professionalism in the reportage of this strange phenomena when the phone rang. It was Ricardo Castanõn.

"Ron, I have something that may interest you," he said. He spoke in his usual soft deep voice, calm and authoritative, a voice that makes every word precious and believable, even if sometimes grammatically imperfect.

"I'm listening."

"There's a statue weeping tears."

"Where?"

"Cochabamba."

"Where?" I asked again hoping he might think I didn't hear him properly the first time.

"Cochabamba. In Bolivia. A journalist he called me. He recorded it on camera for local TV and he knew I have been looking at these cases. So I went. It happened in front of my own eyes."

"When?"

"14 April at 7.56 pm." Typical Ricardo. I was his friend and friends use first names and words like 'typical'.

"First it was clear, like tears and then a large tear of dark red liquid came spontaneously from the left eye and…."

"Was it blood?"

"Well I don't know. I collected it as it had fallen about 6 centimetres as a specimen."

"Were there other witnesses?"

"Seven. We all saw it. Including someone who recorded on video what was happening. And no Ron, there is no way that anyone could have interfered with the statue to produce those effects without us noticing." Friends also enjoy the prerogative of pre-empting the inevitable next question.

"Have you had it tested?"

"Not yet. I thought you might join me, with your camera in New Orleans. We should document the tests and the findings. I want to have it independently tested at GenTest Laboratories. They have a very good reputation according to my enquiries at the State University of Georgia. And," he paused, "the United States is not so Catholic, not like here in South America. Whatever the results are they must be entirely credible."

We met in New Orleans and handed a sample to Dr Anne Montgomery. She was given no prior history of its origin or context. It was to a blind test. In two months we'd have our results. But two months was too long for me to wait. I had to see for myself. So I travelled with my wife, Gabrielle, and Bill Steller, my cameraman friend, to a place on the globe I'd never heard of, to a place which hadn't even existed for me a few weeks ago: Cochabamba.

In the middle of South America is Bolivia, and in the middle of Bolivia is Cochabamba. Its picturesque setting at the foot of the mountains, favourable climate and fertile soil, attracted the original Cechua Indians to settle in the area. In 1542, no doubt additionally attracted by the silver mines, came the Spanish imperialists. And so Cochabamba is, on one hand, a reflection of hundreds of years of Spanish culture, architecture language and religion, and on the other, a colourful legacy to the traditional Cechua Indian presence. Taller even than the famous Christo Redentor on Corcevado in Rio de Janeiro is the gigantic statue of Christ that towers over Cochabamba. And at the foot of the same mountain is a modest house in which was another statue of Christ. This one was only a bust and quite small. This one was bleeding.

It was a delicate sculpture, a bust about thirty centimetres high, made of plaster. It was executed in a realist style and was of little notable artistic merit. The original, from which this one was copied, was known as 'The Christ of Limpias' and, after it reportedly shed blood in a village in Spain in 1919, thousands of cheap plaster copies were made and circulated, principally in the Spanish speaking world.

From a painted crimson mantle draped over the shoulders rises a tormented face with uncannily life-like eyes portraying Jesus' face in agony. Traditionally called the 'Ecce Homo' image, it recalls the moment in Christ's Passion when he was brought back to Pontius Pilate after the brutal scourging by the Roman soldiers. His appearance is so wretched that no one wants to even look at him. Pilate presents him to the crowds to rouse their sympathy with the Latin words, 'Ecce Homo.' (Behold the man!) Remember that he had been stripped, beaten with whips to which metal hooks were attached, and then mocked as a 'king'. A reed was placed in his hands in lieu of a sceptre. A purple cloak was thrown over his naked body, purple being, in ancient times, the colour of royalty. And a helmet of roughly woven thorns was forced onto his head as a crown. This innocent humiliated man, beaten to a bloody pulp, to within an inch of his life, in whom no external beauty remained, was the prototype man, the king of the universe; 'Ecce Homo'.

The statue was placed on a flower bedecked table on one side of a medium sized room The other side was filled with people. Dark streaks followed the contours of the face and encrustations of what certainly appeared to be dried blood lay on the forehead. The upturned eyes and open mouth depicted great physical, guttural suffering, as if the subject was frozen in the act of uttering a mournful cry. Whether it was a hoax or not, it was certainly a most moving sight; gruesome and tragic and unnervingly life-like. Someone aptly said, "The statue seems to be etched in sorrow with

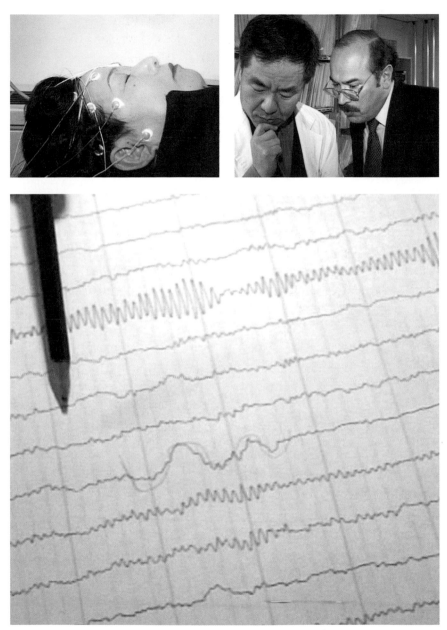

Dr Castanõn performs EEG test on Julia Kim of Korea.
She is seen to produce delta waves

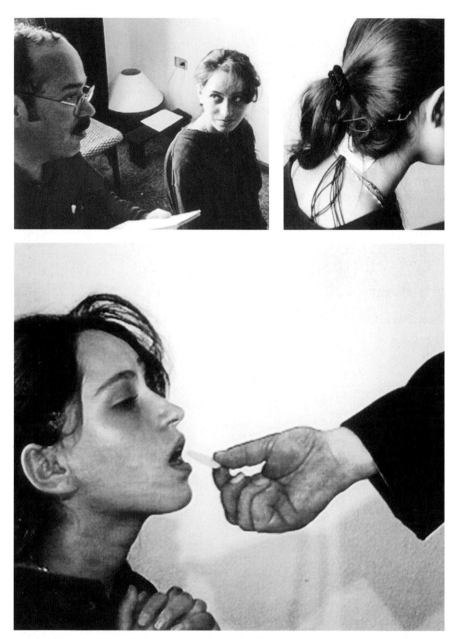

Dr Castañón performs EEG tests on Patricia Talbot of Ecuador
She produced delta waves at the moment of communion

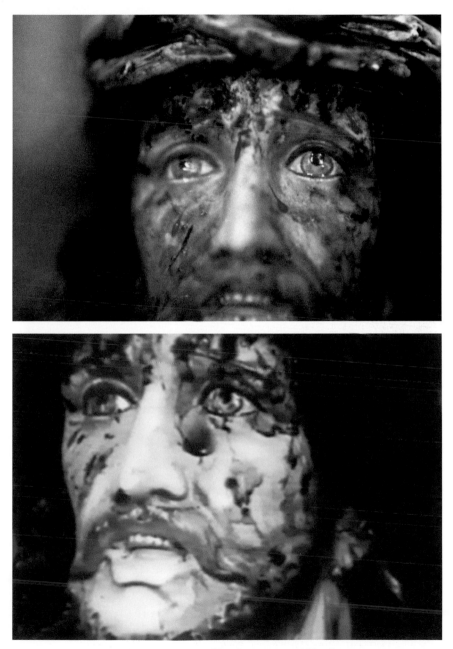

In 1995 the statue is filmed weeping and bleeding

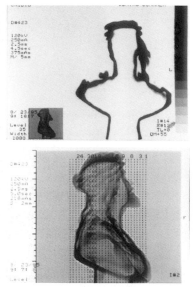

Silvia Arevalo

X-Ray examination shows statue has not been tampered with

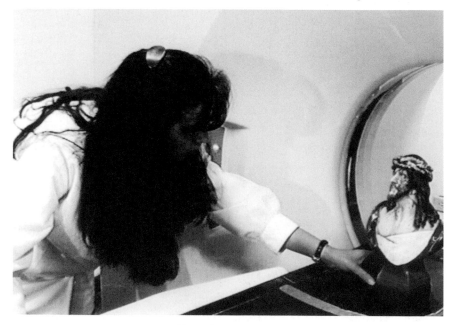

Statue being X-Rayed

Scrapings of "blood" from the statue are taken for examination

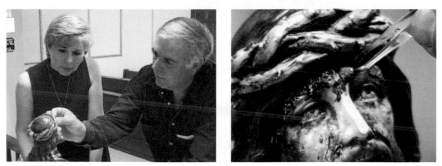

Ron Tesoriero takes sample for testing

Professor Fiori views sample from statue, before testing it (Rome; 1996)

*Dr Robert Lawrence,
Forensic Pathologist (USA)*

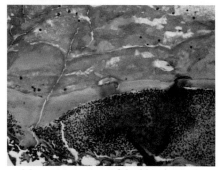

*Microscopic view of the blood sample
containing fragments of stratified
squamous epithelium*

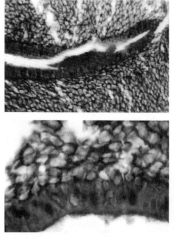

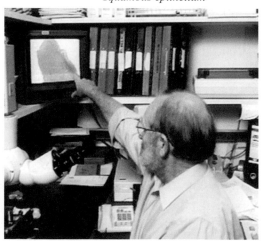

Microscopic photographs of thorn

*Dr John Walker, Sydney University, points at the
cell structure of a thorn in the blood sample*

the paint of its own blood."

Silvia Arevolo, a divorcee in her mid forties and mother of two, was
an airline stewardess. She was the owner of the statue and will never
forget the 9 March 1995 when her life changed forever.

"I went to this shop. I saw they had in the window statues that I did
not like very much. So I went into the store and asked the owner if
he had any other statues of the Virgin Mary. None of what he showed
me I liked. The storekeeper then showed me a statue of the bust of
Jesus of Limpias. I liked it immediately. It was love at first sight. So
this is the one I bought and brought home."

"What did you do with it after you purchased it?" I asked.

"I brought it straight home."

"Was it packaged in any way?"

"The storekeeper wrapped it in newspaper and placed it in a plastic
bag."

"When did you unwrap it?"

"As soon as I got home."

"What did you do then?"

"I started preparing a prayer room. I used to use this room for a
gymnasium, so I had to move many things out. I brought other things
in and moved them around. This took me all afternoon."

"What happened then?"

"At about 7 pm I asked my family to come and see the way I had set
it up and to pray with me. My cousin was also staying with us. When
she came in she asked if someone had been sprinkling water on the
statue. Then she said, 'This cannot be possible!'

We could all see the tears began coming down the face." Silvia took
a deep breath, and when she continued her voice had shifted. "The
emotion and the feeling you get to see God crying is indescribable."
Silvia was the first of fifteen witnesses we interviewed. Some had
seen only the 'tears' form and fall, others had seen 'blood' form into
drops which ran from the eyes and the forehead down the ravaged

cheeks. In three instances a camera had been set up and left to record the spontaneous formation of blood and tears. No human or other interference was detected. Various witnesses had collected samples of the blood on cotton cloths and swabs. We interviewed and filmed them and their declarations. Then, one night, I saw and felt it for myself. Clear liquid welled up in the eyes and fell, like real tears, down the cheeks. With some trepidation I touched the eye and watched the liquid on my finger dry while the statue's eyes remained wet. It was astonishing. Ricardo collected samples of 'tears', 'blood' and 'dried coagulated blood'. We had work to do, and laboratories to visit.

With poignant tenderness, as if lifting a frail child, Silvia's mother picked up the statue, wrapped it in a shawl, and brought it to Dr Castanõn and me in a waiting car. Our destination was Centro Scanners, a medical facility in the city. There the statue elicited tears and awe from the staff who had been following the story of the miraculous statue in the local press. It was placed on a sliding platform and disappeared into the CAT scanner. As I watched this happen I saw a poignant and strange irony. Here, I thought, was the same Christ, portraying wounds and blood from the torture experienced at the hands of men two thousand years ago, being subjected to the inquisitive penetrating radiation of the men of the 20th century. Regardless of the CAT scan results, regardless of any scientific and technological test, would we ever really scratch the surface of his mystery?

Even before the results were out I felt there was no trickery involved. Silvia and her family had been, all along, completely willing to submit to any scientific, ecclesiastical or media investigation. Their homes and their lives were open to both the curious and the pious. No exchange of money was involved. It was all too transparent, too simple and too innocent for fraud.

The X-Ray verdict confirmed my thoughts. The statue was solid plaster moulded around a void of air. If there had been any perforation or hole, "even as fine as the diameter of a human hair," declared the radiologist, it would have been detected. I was strongly inclined to pronounce that what I had witnessed was outside of natural laws and was therefore miraculous.

The GenTest Lab report came back. Results from samples delivered to the Forensic Biology division of the New South Wales Government Department of Public Health also came back. And so did the results from tests conducted on two sets of samples by Professor Angelo Fiori. He was the professor of legal medicine at the Gemelli Hospital in Rome. All confirmed that the samples passed the test for blood. And there was another puzzle shared by all the scientists involved; none of them could fathom why they failed to get a genetic profile from standard DNA analysis, given that the samples provided were ample enough and fresh enough to yield a result. They were all baffled.

"The thing which is very strange, very difficult to explain is that there's no way we can get a DNA profile. All the components are there. It acts like blood. Looks like blood. In chemical and physical composition it's human blood. Yet we can't get the DNA extract"

One said, "It indicated a high molecular weight for human DNA. It's a big mystery I'll tell ya."

Another said, "I have no explanation for this unusual phenomenon."

And yet another said "Impressive phenomena."

One even gave a short lecture: "Reproducibility is the cornerstone of science. You should be able to show its reproducible. Which of course had been shown. It's like saying we have the fact of it being a human hand and yet are unable to discern any fingerprints although we know that we should."

They also said that these were not the results they would expect if someone put their blood on or in a statue. They would have been able to ascertain without doubt the genetic fingerprint of that person.

The sample plucked from the encrustations on the forehead of the statue was tested by Dr Robert Lawrence, a forensic pathologist from San Francisco. It revealed the presence of something completely unforeseen and quite remarkable: epidermal tissue. Human skin.
"As though the blood had been pulled off the face of a person like a scab that takes with it part of the skin. Delicate thin skin; skin that has no thick keratin layer," he explained, "not skin that would come from the palms or soles of the feet or the back, but skin from the face."
When the source of the sample was finally revealed to Dr Lawrence in his office at the lab he responded to camera. "This material could not come from an inanimate object. So either the statue is not a statue or this is some kind of ruse"
The CAT scan results were then thrown into his confusion. "I'm having a hard time in my mind," he said, "deciding what it could be. All I can say is that I find it very amazing. But it must be some kind of deception. But then," he mused, "if it was a deception only blood would be present. Not skin cells as well. It is not within the realm of our understanding. For myself, on a very personal level, I would prefer this to be a trick."

In transit, one of the samples taken from the forehead of the statue had separated into two smaller fragments within the test tube. On the recommendation of a scientist at the NSW Crime Laboratory at Lidcombe, a Mr Goetz, I submitted the second broken fragment of the original sample to Dr Marianne Morgan for a pathological examination. She is a haematologist and oncologist from Gosford. She sent the sample to Douglass Laboratories where it was examined by the pathologist Dr Ian Clark. When his report came back it declared:

'Sections show an autolysed fragment of organic tissue of non-human origin. The material has a definite structure, including nucleated cells. The material is undoubtedly not of human origin.'

At this point I was confused. How could a sample break in half in a test tube and one half pass the presumptive test for human blood (along with the three others collected from the same source), and then this last fragment be something emphatically 'non-human'? What exactly was it? I then sent the enigmatic sample to Dr Peter Ellis, a specialist and lecturer in forensic medicine at the University of Sydney. He conferred with a colleague at the Westmead Hospital regarding the sample and it was this scientist, Dr John Walker, who provided the answer. He agreed to be filmed and interviewed about his finding. Like all the others he had no idea of the origin of what he was seeing under his microscope and which was projected onto a monitor that I could see and film as he pointed and explained:

"I looked at the sample under this microscope. It looks like the cross-section of part of a plant. Very small when you look at it with a naked eye; it's a matter of a millimetre or two in dimension, but in cross-section under the microscope it has a mass of tissue here in the centre; this purple area which is very small plant cells. Now given this structure, this very tight close structure, and the presence of these heavily lined air passages, my feeling is that this is of a 'spine' which grows in a fairly dry sort of area. What it's designed to do is prevent as much fluid loss as possible from this plant tissue so that you have only got these openings to the outside from the lower side and this very waxy surface on the outside to prevent fluid loss."

At this point I couldn't help but interrupt." When you talk about a 'spine' do you mean a 'thorn'?"

"Yes. Yes… The plant that comes to mind is a date palm which has really vicious thorns around the base, or hawthorn. If they stick into you they break off and you get bits of them stuck into you."

I then disclosed to Dr Walker the origin of the sample and the results of the other tests, that it was taken from a bleeding statue and that it was human blood. Along with the other scientists he had no explanation. I had none either. Not about the absence of a genetic profile. Not about why this statue was bleeding human blood. Not about the presence of skin cells or plant tissue like that of a thorn.

Dr Richard Haskell, a histopathologist and cytopathologist from Gosford in New South Wales examined the pathology slides of the blood samples. His expertise lies in identification of cells and cell clusters and he was able to identify those which had puzzled Dr Lawrence. "They are non-keratinized stratified squamous epithelial cells. It is abnormal to find such cells in blood. The admixture seems to indicate that the flesh had been wounded and bled. But the injury," he emphasized, " would not have been caused by a sharp knife or scalpel. A sharp cutting object would sever the flesh and create bleeding but not introduce a multiplicity of epithelial cells stripped of their outer keratin layer. No," he insisted, "the injury was caused by a blow or blows from a crude, blunt object which fractured and traumatized the tissue."

I stared at the microscopic images and was astounded that the story they were revealing had transported me back 2000 years to a brutal scourging with Roman instruments of torture known as flagellum or flagrum. Pellets of lead attached to multiple leather strips repeatedly struck the immobolised victims of this typical and extremely cruel method of punishment. One in particular came to mind. I recollected myself and revealed to Dr Haskell that the source of the samples was inert and inorganic, a plaster statue.

"Could someone have put this tissue on the statue?" I asked

"To do so the person would have had to use something like a serrated saw to cut their skin in tiny pieces and then mix it with blood and then put it on the statue."

Recording the formation of droplets of tears and blood in real time, watching them swell and fall, without human interference was most impressive. The CAT scan proved that no hidden mechanism produced the tears and blood. Multiple laboratory tests confirmed the blood was human, and yet mysteriously resistant to DNA profiling. Traces of plant tissue in the blood were identified as being that of a thorn. Human skin tissue gave a microscopic forensic history of a specific form of injury. All this from a plaster object, a mass-produced unsophisticated image made from crushed stone.

Why?

Although a theologian I consulted didn't offer an all encompassing answer, he did say, with conviction and emphasis, that if these supernatural phenomena were from God then there would be a basis from which to understand them in the Bible. He suggested I look in the Gospel of Luke relating the events just prior to the Crucifixion. Jesus is described in Chapter 19 as triumphantly entering Jerusalem seated on a donkey. The crowds cheered him exultantly, laying their cloaks down in his pathway and waving palms. These were same crowds who had seen and experienced his teaching, his miracles and his healing.

'They cried out
"Blessed is he who is coming
as King in the name of the Lord
Peace in heaven
And glory in the highest heaven"

Some Pharisees in the throng, those who rejected Jesus and felt threatened by his influence, said to him, *"Master reprove your disciples." But he answered, "I tell you if these keep silent, the stones will cry out." As he drew near and came in sight of the city he shed tears over it and said, "If you too had only recognised on this day, the way to Peace! But in fact it is hidden from your eyes."*
Was there a prophetic undertone for our times, in the words of Jesus? Was this little statue in Cochabamba proclaiming God because today we no longer do?

What was obvious was the religious and specifically Catholic iconography of this statue. The world is full of fine sculpture with infinitely greater artistic merit than this little one. Why weren't statues of Winston Churchill or Benjamin Franklin or Saddam Hussein or Julius Caesar or Gandhi or Buddha exhibiting 'behaviour' possible only to the living? I would have had to be blind or stupid not to realise that these 'signs' had a common denominator: something or Someone was pointing, repeatedly, at this man called Jesus, this man who claimed to be one with God and who was made to suffer brutally for it.

My questions were not long in being answered for a short while later Ricardo told me about another case he was working on. A humble housewife claimed to be receiving messages in the form of dictation from Jesus. She, it turned out, had the key to my understanding the mystery of the statue in Bolivia.

CHAPTER 5

THE
SECRETARY

"I am a common and ordinary woman. I was an office clerk, and now a housewife and I, unworthy as I am, have suddenly become the secretary of the Lord, I who never knew anything about Theology or read the Bible (I shamefully admit this now that I am starting to read it), all of a sudden start to learn of the Love of my God, who is also yours."

So says Katya or Catalina Rivas of herself. She is an ordinary woman, a grandmother, quite matronly, who becomes luminously beautiful when she speaks of her Divine companion. She speaks only Spanish and never completed high school and yet, to her own astonishment and bewilderment, at the age of 48 she began writing, without theological error, hundreds of pages of profound teaching and biblical commentary which she says are dictated to her by Jesus himself. The historical definition of a prophet, it must be remembered, comes from the Hebrew word, 'navi' translated as, 'one who is called.' In Sacred Scripture a prophet is one who is a mouthpiece called to convey God's will. He or she is not, as current thought seems to insist, preoccupied with foretelling the future.

Katya has now 'written' 14 books, compilations of the messages she receives. They include sophisticated passages in Greek, Latin and Polish, languages she cannot speak, read, write or understand. And I have to say, that these writings are some of the most inspiring and informative works on the Catholic faith that I have ever read. I am not alone in this appraisal. Theological experts, including Bishop Rene Fernandez of Cochabamba, have declared them to be free of doctrinal or moral error and so her work carries the imprimatur of the Roman Catholic Church.

One particular message detailing Jesus' reflections on the mystery of his suffering and its redemptive value struck me forcefully in the context of the strange phenomenon of the bleeding statue.

"I have taken as a symbol a piece of wood, a cross. I have carried it with great love for the good of all. I have suffered real affliction so that everybody could be joyful with me. But today, how many believe in him who truly loved you and loves you? Contemplate me in the image of the Christ who cries and bleeds. There and in this way the world has me." [1]

Once again I was fascinated and she, gracious and obliging, permitted me to film her in the process of writing. This is what happens: She starts on a blank page, writes one sentence, then another, then a paragraph, then another, all without the slightest hesitation, correction or alteration, and without reference to any other books. Unlike the rest of us, she never stops to consider the form or content of the text, never seems to search for a word. It's as if she's operating on auto-pilot, although she is not in any sort of ecstatic state and is fully aware of all that is going on around her.

On one occasion she wrote in this uncanny fashion non-stop for almost an hour as I filmed. What for me clearly demonstrated that the writings were not the product of a photographic memory or plagiarism was that I saw and filmed Katya write complex, detailed and informative responses to questions posed by witnesses present at the time of her writing. In these circumstances she had no prior notice of the subject matter being discussed.

It is difficult to select and present in a few pages extracts from Katya's numerous writings that would do justice to their content. In what follows you can see how Jesus endears his listeners to appreciate who He is and the love that He has for us.

"Look at your pen. For Me you are My pen that I use to trace the symbols that express My words. What your hand writes guided by Mine will remain. Repeated and amplified by other voices it will fill the earth. [2]

I have created the world and also the tree that was to provide the wood for My cross. I created the bramble bush that was to provide the thorns for My royal crown. I buried in the bowels of the earth the iron that was to forge My nails.... When I came in person to visit My land there was no room for Me in the inns of the world. It was a cold, freezing world that night when I came to mankind. I came to men but men did not recognize Me. There was no room for Me. And now?

Everything, The heavens and the earth and all that inhabit them are Mine. Only the love of My creatures is not Mine. And that is what I search for.

I am suffering. The world is no longer Mine because it has strayed from Me. I am alone. Alone..... Where is love, true love? Sincere and unselfish. I want the heart of man. You will write in capital letters that JESUS FIRST AND FOREMOST WANTS MEN'S HEARTS AND THEN ALL THE REST." [3]

As I was to become aware of with my encounter with Father Aliprandi, we as Christians are often reminded of the promise that Jesus makes in the Bible, "ask and though shalt receive." This is perhaps a difficult concept for us to come to terms with, that God is there listening to us when we pray, ready to give us what we ask of Him.

Katya is filmed writing under dictation from Jesus on a number of occasions

Jesus addresses the subject of prayer in many of Katya's writings.

"There has never been anyone who has placed his faith in Me and has been abandoned. He who prays to Me with faith, obtains all he has asked for. When the graces asked for are spiritual and useful to the soul, be sure that you will receive them. That is why I have taught you that when you ask for a grace, you should call Me Father, so you will turn to Me with the same faith with which a son turns to his father who loves him.

If you heed the promise I have made you, of listening to he who prays, who can doubt that I will break My promise? I am not like men who promise and do not keep their promise, either because they are lying when they make a promise, or change their minds after they have made their promise. I cannot lie because I am the Truth; I cannot change, because I am justice, rectitude, and know the consequences of what I do. How can I fail to keep My promises to you? (4)

Therefore, let your prayer be the key to opening the coffer of My Heart that is not locked up as you may think, but is instead wide open to all of you . Pray generously , always, and at all times , according to what your duties allow. Let it be a happy occasion as you are united to me . Do not make me listen to the sound of numerous words which resemble the noise of broken plates ready to be thrown away . Instead , your prayer should be like the jingling of fine glasses that I myself would like to fill with divine nectar. (5)

As immortal King of the centuries and Supreme Lord of everything that exists, My power is made available for mankind's disposal; it is enough only to ask for it lovingly. (6)

Words and their definitions are tools of trade of the legal system, and as a person within that system, I had laboured at precise definitions, ambiguities and interpretations all my working life. The word 'neighbour' may be a simple noun, but in law, the religious dictum to love your neighbour becomes instead to not injure your neighbour. Who exactly your neighbour is, is a difficult concept in law and is often, in the end, the subject of contention amongst lawyers. What I was encountering in the writings of Katya was so refreshingly simple. This definition caught my eye:

"A friend is one who inconveniences himself, who deprives himself of something or of many things to offer them to you. A friend is one who will give up his time of rest for you. A friend is he who can in a moment give up the comfort of his home so as to make you feel comfortable, loved and appreciated. A friend is one who leaves his land to help you save yours. A friend is he who confides his sorrows and his joys, who is always transparent with you and who always takes you toward growth in faith and love of God.

A friend is he who builds, who unites, who gathers, not one who tears apart, who destroys, knocks down, so he can sit on top of the rubble. A friend is he who gives his life to save you...as I did." [7]

Consider in the examples which follow that the writer has a rudimentary education, a limited functional vocabulary, no theological training, and humble social standing. Consider also that these are tiny glimpses of extensive treatises on a variety of teachings. They have been translated from Spanish, the language in which they were dictated to Katya by Jesus. Various translators have remarked on how beautiful and almost lyrical the words are in Spanish, and that they often found it difficult to reproduce that same poetry with English words

"I gave you spring; nevertheless, its flowers have a short life. I gave you the perfume of the flowers and it also passes, but not as quickly as the flowers from which it comes. In everything I have left something that testifies to the invisible, and this is what matters most

because whilst it acknowledges the present life it gives an assurance of a future life. . What is a rose bud? Is it only what you see and nothing more?.... What is the perfume of a flower? Is it just something that delights man's sense of smell?... It is in fact, a diffusing of unacknowledged vitality that I have put in all plants as a testimony of My Spirit that infuses existence – life. [8]

Here I found a theme repeated throughout the Bible and the history of the Church:

I choose the smallest and most useless things of the world to confuse the great ones of this century. The more inadequate the instrument seems for the job, the more skill I use to manage it, and thus everything will serve for the accomplishment of my designs of Love

I have said it before; I want to be presented to the modern world like Joseph who opens the Pharaoh's granaries and distributes the grain in abundance so that there will be no hungry people on earth. I would like to be presented like the prodigal son's father who, aged by the pain of his son's absence, keeps watch from a window with a small light of hope for the return of his beloved son. I live among all of you in the air you breathe, the water you drink, and the bread you eat, with all the grandiose work of creation that never ceases. In this manner I am among you all, alive, real, with the perpetual sacrifice of the Cross and the glory of resurrection in each Eucharist.

I want the world to know that God is unchanging, that He never lessens his love for men; I need for man to know that I never set limits to my forgiveness and that I do not ask the prodigal son how he has squandered my estate, nor do I ask for an account of his wickedness. It is a new mercy that I want to give to this new generation. [9]

I had always wondered who or what exactly was 'poor in spirit'. I couldn't understand. I assumed to be rich in spirit meant to be very spiritual and therefore better than being poor in spirit. In this message I found rest for my curiosity.

We shall talk about the "poor in spirit". I said, "Blessed are the poor in spirit". Actually, the meaning of these words in Hebrew is blessed are those who lack arrogance. The significance of this phrase has been misinterpreted. These words are meant to imply not that I praise solely those unattached to earthly goods but instead, to exalt the humble. (10)

In the Bible Jesus so often teaches using themes drawn from agricultural life. I recognized the same person speaking in the following message.

Imagine that you were poor peasants tired and hungry coming back to your humble house in the fields, where, apart from a little rest and a poor meal, you could expect nothing else. Imagine if in the midst of your fatigue, one night, instead of returning to a poor and modest home you find an unimaginable palace, an incomparable gift given to you by a magnanimous king, as a gesture of altruism.
Well then, this is how it will be for you at the end of your lives. On your last day, already set by Me, you will do the things that I have assigned to you, and as usual, you will pass by Me, tired and perhaps sad, aiming to find rest; to soothe some pain, to overcome some sadness or any other human concern. You will pass by Me, and direct your step towards reaching the highest goal that you had hoped to achieve for yourself that day without suspecting that I have already determined the end of your fatigue and that your own dismal house down here, is to be turned, on that same day, into a divine dwelling, even if for some, by way of passing through Purgatory.
At the end of your journey, your eyes will open to see the divine

Alcazar, in which I, the Love that is speaking to you dwell amid a thousand delights.

What a marvellous change will take place on that day! How easy will it be to love Me, the object of your desires! And how willingly, if necessary, will you go to purify yourselves among the purifying souls! You, the peasants, shall be transformed into nobility by My Grace, and will see how everything is changed, how the reality of Heaven was, is and will be the true and sole goal of every pilgrim.

Courage, children, courage! For there is in Heaven a Mother waiting for you. Courage! For your Jesus is in Heaven, waiting for you to reward you all.

Courage and patience because in Heaven, above all the holy creatures that I have mentioned, is your God, Who loves His souls with an infinite love, and by comparison any other love is but a tiny spark.

Courage! for in Heaven everything will be restful and your hearts will be filled with joy.

Come then all of you who are listening to Me and you shall see how impossible it is on earth to describe holy Paradise. [11]

To the question that might be asked, "how can we know that the words Katya writes are from God", Jesus answers with these words:-

It is an unfathomable mystery that I may want to manifest Myself through a creature to the man of today... How many human mysteries you come to know only by their fruits, from their effects! You do not doubt , because you see their effects even though you do not see the causes. Well, the mystery is that the effects can be perceived, acknowledged as authentic because it produces movement of souls towards Me ,which is its guarantee. My Words are the same. More over, I have been repeating them throughout the ages to dozens of children and there are still many who do not recognise Me, who analyse, who look for faults... How blind are they! [12]

It was a remarkable experience for me to see and film the mystic as scribe to a supernatural voice. It may have been the first time such amazing scenes have been filmed, but it certainly was not the first time it had happened. The spiritual library of the Church has records of many such instances, some of which form significant corroboration of Catholic doctrine.

St Catherine of Sienna is a case in point. She was an illiterate, extremely holy woman from the 14th century who received profound dictation from Jesus. These writings are regarded by the Church as so valuable, that it posthumously conferred on her the honour of being a 'Doctor of the Church'. This declaration, coming from the Pope, is rare; only thirty three 'teacher' saints have been declared 'Doctor'. Other saints in that same category include St John of the Cross, St Teresa of Avila, St Alphonsus Liguori, and St Thomas Aquinas. However brilliant their writings, however astonishing their supernatural charisms, the Doctors of the Church were not sanctified for their written contributions. They were first and foremost recognized as heroically virtuous, for living exemplary lives of selflessness and love.

(1)   The Passion
(2)   The Crusade of Love (19)
(3)   Door to Heaven (13)
(4)   Door to Heaven (38)
(5)   The Crusade of Mercy (88)
(6)   The Ark of the New Covenant (102)
(7)   From Sinai to Calvary
(8)   The Crusade of Love (18)
(9)   The Crusade of Love (160)
(10)   The Crusade of Mercy (123)
(11)   The Crusade of Mercy (151)
(12)   The Crusade of Salvation (20)

CHAPTER 6

THE
STIGMATIST

On 14 September 1224, while in ecstatic prayer on Mt Alverna, the five bleeding wounds of Christ crucified appeared on the hands, feet and side of St Francis of Assisi. They continued to bleed and he continued to suffer the accompanying physical pain until he died two years later. Jesus told him, *"I have given you the stigmata which are the emblems of my Passion, so that you may be my standard-bearer."*

In the centuries that followed many individuals were reported to have borne the stigmata, the rare and unusual insignia of wounds which bleed spontaneously and cause immense physical suffering. In some, the wounds were invisible. They involved excruciating pain but no physical lesions. Such was the case with St Catherine of Sienna. Some were marked with only the wound in the side. Others with only the puncture wounds of the crown of thorns. Some stigmatics exhibited bleeding wounds for years, and others only at certain times of the year.

In the first half of the twentieth century two women are well documented as manifesting mystical phenomena including stigmata. In 1925 Therese Neumann, received the wounds which eloquently corresponded to those of Christ. They persisted until her death in 1962. She reportedly experienced bilocation, visions, ecstasies and raptures and allegedly ate no food and drank no liquid her entire adult life. Rose Fenelon, "Little Rose" a native of Quebec, also experienced stigmata from 1927 until her early death in 1931.

The most famous contemporary stigmatic was an Italian Capuchin priest, Padre Pio who had persistent painful bleeding wounds for nearly fifty years. This is a fact beyond dispute, a fact corroborated by repeated examinations of the lesions by various doctors, and by the many thousands of faithful who flocked to attend his daily celebration of the Mass, where despite the great effort taken to conceal them, the continuously flowing blood penetrated through bandages and gloves. Other wounds he sustained, like when he cut his fingers with a knife, healed and left normal scars. Yet the wounds of the stigmata persisted. When they did finally heal shortly before his death in 1968 not a trace of their ever having existed remained. There was not even the slightest blemish let alone a scar.

Padre Pio showed no interest in explaining his stigmata. He accepted his very unusual physical suffering with humility and even embarrassment. Though dramatic, he believed it was a minor incidental to his real struggle which was to live a holy life in conformity with Christ and his Church. When people suggested that the stigmata were caused by his excessive concentration on the passion of Christ he responded, "Go out to the fields and look very closely at a bull. Concentrate on him with all your might and see if you start to grow horns."

In 2002, at the official canonization of Padre Pio, Pope John Paul II said, "His stigmata were the work and sign of divine mercy, which redeemed the world by the cross of Christ. Those open bleeding wounds spoke of God's love for everyone. In God's plan the cross consitutes the true instrument of salvation for the whole of humanity and the way explicitly proposed by the Lord to all those who wish to follow Him."

Like St Francis, Padre Pio received the stigmata during the octave of the 14 September when the Church commemorates the finding of the true cross in 326. The significance of this date warrants a brief historical excursion:

For the first three centuries Christians suffered intense persecution at the hands of the ruling Roman Empire. Thousands were brutally martyred for their religion, an underground organisation operating in defiance of the official worship of multiple pagan gods. Then in 312, the Emperor Constantine himself underwent a dramatic conversion precipitated by a mystical experience. On the eve of an imminent battle against his rival Maxentius, 'he saw with his own eyes the trophy of a cross of light in the heavens, above the sea, and bearing the inscription Conquer By This. At this sight he was struck with amazement, and his whole army also, which followed him on his expedition and witnessed the miracle.' (Medieval Sourcebook: Eusebius: Conversion of Constantine)

Shortly afterwards he had a vision in which Christ directed him to make on his standard, a likeness of the cross he had seen. Constantine complied and won an unforseen victory to secure his political position. His conversion resulted in an era of tolerance for Christianity and eventually to the Christianisation of all of Europe. Wanting to discover more about the cross Constantine sent his mother, Helena, an enthusiastic elderly convert, on a pilgrimage to Jerusalem. On her orders excavations at the site of Jesus' crucifixion unearthed three crosses and the 'titulus', the inscription Pilate ordered nailed to Jesus' cross. It was written in three languages: Aramaic, Latin and Greek. What was fascinating, was that the Aramaic (Hebrew) text was written correctly, that is from right to left, but the other languages were written incorrectly and read backwards, that is also from right to left. The writer of the titulus was clearly schooled only in his own written language. Such an oversight could not have been forged.

At the nearby site of the resurrection she demolished a shrine to

Venus built to deliberately conceal the sepulchre below. There, on Constantine's orders, a magnificent Basilica of the Holy Sepulchre was built to venerate the cross and the resurrection. The dedication was a solemn ceremony lasting eight days in imitation of the dedication of the Jewish Temple. This octave of the 14 September was the first Christian octave in history instituted expressly to venerate the cross and resurrection.

In St Francis and Padre Pio we see that God chooses people to exhibit the wounds of Jesus. That he does so in concordance with dates of significance in Church history was a discovery I was to encounter again.

In 1996 I received news from Bolivia. Katya Rivas had received the stigmata. The written messages and the weeping statue were one thing. This was quite another. Or so it seemed to me at the time. Maybe I had bitten off more than I could chew. That Christ's 'secretary' now exhibited his own wounds was a dramatic endorsement of the messages she was receiving and the power over the natural world wielded by their source. Now, it seemed to me, the true Author was sealing the correspondence with his signature.

I felt the whole world should know about this. The stigmata was a reality, factual in every way, more real probably than what passes for news on our media. I wanted to reach the biggest possible audience through the medium the world most loved: television. But I was an amateur filmmaker. I needed help if I was to have any chance of realising my somewhat grandiose ambition of sharing what I was witnessing. I didn't want to tell people what was happening, I wanted them to see for themselves. And as 'luck' would have it help was not far away. I had no further to look than over my own garden fence.

CHAPTER 7

THE TELEVISION CELEBRITY

My neighbour was Mike Willesee. To me he was a friend, a man with a really big heart. To the rest of Australia he was a big TV star, one of our most respected television journalists, and a famous household name. With a career spanning more than thirty years he had gained a reputation as a hard-hitting news reporter. Renowned for his relentless energy he researched, produced, wrote, interviewed and faced audiences on camera. He never backed down. He went after anyone anywhere to get at the truth and was known for being, in the words of Channel 7, "a good man to have on your side". Every night his face was beamed across the nation as the creator, anchor and producer of an investigative program called 'A Current Affair'. What he said, what he chose to investigate, what his cameras showed reached millions of people. When he spoke people listened. And more than that, they trusted him. For me it was like needing a portrait painted of my wife and knowing that my neighbour was Leonardo da Vinci.

I approached him with the story of the Bolivian stigmatist and my curiosity about what was happening in Cochabamba, knowing that he had little sympathy with anything outside of the hard facts of reality and even less with religious matters. He was a Catholic who had given away his faith, another like my earlier self, who found little that was real or relevant in religion. But his was not so much a drifting from the church as mine had been but a distinct turning away.

Mike Willesee

Mike's father was a working class family man, loyal to the Catholic Church and to the Australian Labour Party. He wore these two allegiances comfortably and they were for him as compatible as the two sleeves of a coat. His politics saw him rise to the top and he became the Minister of Foreign Affairs in the Labour government. But Australia in the fifties was not immune from the McCarthyism which tore into the liberty and mindset of many Americans. Seeing subversive communists behind every bush and a red under every bed became as much a national pastime in Australia as it was in the United States. It even insinuated itself into the minds of certain priests, one of whom went so far as to paint Mike's father's politics as too left and from the pulpit labelled him a Communist. The calumny soon spread and Mike, as a Catholic schoolboy, became a target of vituperative bullying at high school, not so much by the other pupils, but by a few malicious school masters. Feeling fully justified with righteous indignation he turned his back on those responsible, the narrow minded priests and teachers, by rejecting them and the Church they represented.

As his career in television took off he eventually thought no more about it or them. He was smart, an indefatigably resourceful worker whose energy in producing news items and documentaries catapulted him to the very top of the broadcast industry. He became famous and rich. His life was packed with adventure: reporting from war zones around the globe and mixing with the world's newsmakers, with heads of state and the entertainment industry's darlings. He needed nothing more to complete his very public and enormously successful life.

Being a rational, unimpressionable man with both feet planted firmly on the facts of the matter, Mike was naturally skeptical at my revelations about what was happening in Bolivia and said, "Look Ron, these things can't happen and don't happen."
"But it's true though," I countered, "and if we could, if you could, only investigate it the way you do best, it would be the first time ever that the whole world will see it actually happening. Imagine seeing a real stigmatic event in real time?"
"You mean go all the way to some unknown godforsaken place in the middle of Bolivia to see if a crazy woman's hands bleed on cue?"
"Godforsaken," I mumbled, "maybe not."
"It's all mind over matter, or a kind of self-hypnosis or psychosomatic hysteria or a couple of religious fanatics needing some attention and getting up to tricks."
"If it is, then expose it as such. There's a story in that surely?"
"Listen Ron, I've done stories like these before. Remember the one about the Filipino faith healers making a buck by pulling chicken guts out of some poor guy's abdomen. Charlatans exploiting the ignorant! Or the waterfall that was miraculously curing people in

New Zealand? I'm sorry, but I've done this stuff before and it's always a big con. And do you know what the first sign is that it's a fraud? They won't allow anyone to examine their claims closely, with cameras or with scientific tests or with whatever it takes. And," he continued forcefully, " somewhere along the line there's always money involved."

His mind was set. But I wasn't giving up. I persisted saying,

"Look, Mike, you hear me talking about all these things and without even a modicum of consideration you reject them out of hand. You're negative before you know the truth."

"Not negative, just real. Been there, done that. Don't expect me to believe because you believe."

"All of Australia values your opinion on all sorts of issues. You've got a world-class reputation for integrity. You always do a thorough investigation and present an honest evaluation, and so," I paused to add weight to my closing argument, "prove me wrong!"

CHAPTER 8

THE
GOOD THIEF

The 'good man to have on your side' was right by my side, in a Boeing 747, over a vast expanse of Pacific Ocean as we flew to South America. True to form he had taken up the challenge. Uncomfortable questions and the opinions of others, whether or not they were the majority, and whether or not they appeared totally outrageous, were not an obstacle. As always he was championing the underdog. Truth itself was almost always the underdog.

"Why are you doing this?" I asked.
"What do you mean, why?" he replied giving me a quizzical look.
"I mean why are you willing to be dragged to the ends of the earth by a nagging neighbour. Is it to prove me wrong?"
"I don't really know….. I mean I think I know but I'm not sure."
"It's not just about me, is it? It's not me that you're needing to prove wrong. It's more than that, isn't it?"
"Maybe." He replied and settled into the stillness of his own thoughts. Then, hesitating, he continued solemnly. "I have been in some pretty hairy situations in my life. Quite terrifying actually. I've been shot at; felt the bullets whizzing past my ear as I ran and scrambled for cover. I've been arrested in places where the jails are legendary hell holes. I've had to jump out of a chopper into a full-on battlefield, mortar exploding around me, knowing that if I stuffed up the timing it was all over. I've stared down the barrel of a gun and been forced, by the VC in Vietnam, into a jungle so dense you couldn't see two feet in front of you. There've been multiple

forced landings. And yet," he paused in his recount, " I've never been afraid, I mean truly afraid for my life. I don't mean I wasn't scared. It's just that I never thought 'this is it, mate, it's all over'. But then….,"

Mike always looks you in the eye when he speaks but at that moment he turned away slightly to stare out the window at the black night thousands of feet above ground.

"…. one day it was different. It was a couple of months ago. I was in Nairobi. I'd chartered a plane to take us, myself and the camera crew, to the Southern Sudan, into the civil war zone, and we were on the runway about to take off when I just got this overwhelming instinct to cancel it. No, actually, it wasn't instinct. It wasn't a feeling. It wasn't even fear really. No voices in my head or that sort of thing. I just knew. I knew that something bad was going to happen. In all my years I hadn't ever experienced anything like it; a kind of absolute knowing that something terrible was going to happen. I told myself I was being stupid. I was doing what I'd done hundreds of times before. And anyway how could I bale out now? What would I say to my cameraman who'd been through plenty of 'real' danger with me? There was nothing to even worry about on this trip. All the gear was loaded, there were also a couple of people we'd offered a lift to who were waiting, and so I didn't do anything and the plane took off. But that knowing didn't go away and I did something I haven't done in thirty, maybe, forty years." Mike went quiet and far away. "I prayed." I waited for him to continue but he was absorbed in the memory.

"And?" I prompted.

"I said, 'I put myself in your hands, Lord.' "

"And?"

"The whole plane just fell out of the sky. A complete write-off. Wrecked. Pieces of it were all over the place. It never flew again. ….Not one of us was even slightly injured."

He sipped his drink and said no more.

The hours of the flight passed. He didn't appear to be praying, to my immense relief, and our plane, thank God, landed perfectly safely in Buenos Aires. The airport was chaotic and we made our way through the bustle to change for our flight to Bolivia. The check-in area was too small for the crowd of human traffic and haphazard queues of people criss-crossed and jostled one another in a hot and noisy confusion. Getting through airports in third world countries was nothing new to Mike and he remained calm and confident. He came prepared, as one would expect of someone who'd been doing this all his working life. He had with him his much-travelled wallet with the essentials: passports, tickets, contact details and $15 000 in cash.

In one merciless microsecond it vanished, snatched clean out of his backpack.

"It's gone!" Mike gasped, pointing to a woman disappearing into the crowd.

"What's gone? What's wrong? What's going on?" I asked suddenly quite panicked by the look in my friend's face and the changed tone of his voice.

"Everything," he groaned. "Wallet, passports, tickets, money, the lot!"

"Did you see anyone?"

"A woman, I think. There was a woman just then who bumped into me. Now that I remember it was quite suspicious. I did catch a glimpse of her. I'd recognise her again." He was scanning the endless mass of people for a beacon of recognition.

"Let's see if we can find her."

Then Mike pleaded softly, "Not now Jesus, not now. Any other time but not now."

"Mike," I urged, "she's probably getting away. Let's go."

"No, it's no use. By now she's already passed it over to her sidekick. She's a pro. She'll have nothing on her and the next thing we'll be facing cops in a South American jail for accosting an innocent woman."

I felt sick at the thought, but even more sick as the realization dawned that our whole trip was essentially over before it began. Everything had fallen apart. Without that wallet we had no money, no contacts and no easy way out of Argentina.

My head felt heavy and slumped to my chest. I sighed. Straightening up I could see a young woman making straight for us like an arrow seeking its target. Her eyes narrowed grimly as she approached. Unflinching she handed over the wallet to Mike, turned and disappeared in the crowd. Shock, dismay, panic, fear, disbelief, despondency and then sheer exultant relief: I don't think I've ever gone through the entire range of extreme emotions in a single minute ever before. My heart was racing. I needed to sit down.
"Mike check it!" I ordered. "Check the cash. Is it there?"
"No," he said, almost vehemently, "I don't need to."
And he didn't. And it was.
And I was becoming almost certain that all I was doing was acting on behalf of the most powerful client of all. Nothing, absolutely nothing was impossible for Him.

CHAPTER 9

PERFUME
AND BLOOD

The first shot I got of Mike in Bolivia was him stepping off the plane chewing gum. Later he met Ricardo. A joke was exchanged and it sealed their friendship from the beginning. Mike not only really liked him but admired the way he made things happen efficiently and on time but without pretensions to any leadership role. Ricardo always got the ball rolling.

A pot-holed dirt road led to Katya's house. It had no garden, no entrance as such, and faced an empty field. I filmed the meeting. Mike was annoyed that I had compromised his stated intention to be an invisible observer, nothing more than a fly on the wall, by introducing him to Katya as a journalist with questions to ask. He had no questions. Not yet. And the ones he made up on the spot were facile and insincere and deserved the reproach they received. She muttered, uncharitably, "Typical journalist."

Mike then met Father Renzo Sessolo, a priest of the Salesian Order, who was appointed by the Church in 1997 to be Katya's spiritual director. He was there to assist, guide and accompany her on any journeys out of the country and on the more crucial spiritual journey she had accepted. After all she was an ordinary woman through whom and to whom extraordinary and bewildering things were happening. Mike's assessment of him coincided with mine. He was an exceptionally humble, self-effacing man with nothing to prove.

We were returning from Candalaria, a site which held significant memories for Katya as the place where as a child she became aware for the first time of the Virgin Mary as real.

"So what do you think?" I asked Mike.

"I'm not entirely sure. Something's different from the other stories I've investigated."

"You mean Katya's authentic?"

"Well I don't really know. But one thing's for sure: she's not selling anything. There's no money involved. I mean no one's making anything out of this if it's true. Which is very different from all the others."

"No. Her home is modest. Probably very modest by our standards."

"And from my experience I'd say she's not playing to the cameras or us, so I don't think it's about needing special attention. No ulterior motive I can work out."

"I'm impressed by her reverence and concentration when she's at Mass. She's humble. And holy."

"I can't really talk about holiness but she is totally focused and very prayerful, although everybody at Mass seems pretty prayerful to me. She could be putting on one of the most credible performances I've ever seen though, so I'll hold my judgement on that. There's that other thing, though, and it's really got me stumped."

"What thing?"

"This," he said and pulled out a white handkerchief.

"Is that the same one you gave to Katya?"

"Yeah. I don't know if you noticed, but all day long she was wiping the palms of her hands, as if they were worrying her and then I saw the priest sneaking her tissues which she used to wipe off the wetness."

"It's been a long hot day," I said reversing my role as advocate for divine manifestation.

"But that's the funny thing. I was watching her really, really closely. She wasn't perspiring. Not on her face. But there was wetness coming from her hands. Only her hands. And after she dried them on the tissues she'd hand back the sodden ones to Father Renzo. Then when we were in the church I think he ran out and I could see she was looking pretty agitated so I offered her one. She gave it back. And well….. I was amazed. Absolutely amazed."

"Why, because she gave it back?" I returned wryly.

"No, because of the fragrance. I smelt it and it smelled fantastically beautiful. Like nothing I'd ever smelt before. Definitely not man-made perfume; somehow completely natural. And definitely not perspiration! I just don't know. I can't think of anything to explain it rationally. But it was," and he hesitated, searching for the right word, "out of this world. Sublime, maybe. More beautiful than anything I've ever smelt before. If there's anything that makes me think there's something supernatural going on it's this."

He looked long at the square of white cotton then carefully folded it and put it in his shirt pocket, next to his heart.

There was still the other matter to explore and it was the one which so often brands Catholicism as a haven for hysterical ignorant fanatics. I suspected that Mike was thinking that on this one there would be no contest, that some simple science would crush the gullible believers and the crafty magicians seducing them with party tricks. It was the issue of the bleeding statue. We entered Silvia's house. A crowd of people were gathered around the statue.

"What's the matter, Ron? Mike asked.

"I don't know. I'm not sure."

"It's a pretty shocking sight. Looks so real and so,…so brutal."

"It's not that. It's that it's, well, it's changed."

"You haven't seen it for nearly a year."

"I know. But it's not all the stuff on it I'm talking about. The face itself seems to have changed. The actual features look different. The expression is more agonized. The eyes have rolled back and the mouth is somehow more horribly contorted. I swear the whole thing has changed."

"Yeah, well we've had a lot going on that's pretty weird and I think you've had enough for one day. Let's go, mate. There's no tears, no blood coming out. Nothing's happening. Maybe it did, maybe not. Enigmatic, sure, vividly tragic, but I don't quite get what it's all for, if it's for real. Although I'd have to say that the lab reports intrigue me. Why they all say they can't get a DNA profile despite the fact that they should easily be able to."

"It's about pain and suffering," I said. "His."

Leaving Bolivia I was, I admit, a little downcast. My friend had not been convinced that anything fundamentally Divine was taking place. He was intrigued, but not hooked. My disappointment lay in my friend's reaction but even more in having to admit that maybe I'd set my target too high in hoping that Mike would have been interested in examining the claims about this statue. I wanted the story to be bigger than I could ever make it, as big as only someone like Mike could make it by throwing the clout of his experience and celebrity behind the strange happenings in Bolivia. Perhaps I failed to understand how huge the collateral damage would be to a media star's career should he dare to endorse anything other than the prevailing godless secular world view. Perhaps I hadn't quite considered what complete conversion entails for one whose life glitters under public glare. There was nothing further I could do or say. So I waited. Prayed a little and trusted a little more.

CHAPTER 10

MY
MOTHER

Bartolomea Famularo, known to everyone as Bertha, was born of immigrant parents in New York in 1912. They had come from the Aeolian Islands off the coast of Sicily in their youth. She married Antonino Tesoriero, my father, in Sydney in 1932 and bore four boys. She enjoyed robust health until late in 1998, when at the age of 86 she collapsed with a stroke and was hospitalized. We all believed that her end had come. She was given the last rites.

I was in turmoil since I had invited Katya Rivas, Dr Castanõn and Father Renzo to Sydney. I was swamped with the work of promoting and organizing speaking engagements for them and in the middle of it all, my mother became critically ill. I was torn, wanting to be in two places at once. I was preoccupied with my documentary work and the imminent arrival of my Bolivian guests. That the lift was slow at the Mater Misericordia Hospital added to my frustration. In the foyer, next to these lifts, was a bust of Christ. I was moved to pray.
"Jesus, I have been looking after your mother, please look after mine."
The lift arrived and I went up. My mother didn't look good.

Two days later Gabrielle and I were entertaining our foreign visitors. After lunch I suggested we drop by the hospital to visit my mother on our way home. I dropped Katya and Gabrielle off at the entrance and went off to park the car. Gabrielle gave this account

Bertha receives miraculous host

Father Renzo blesses Bertha with holy oil

of what happened when they walked into the reception area of the hospital.

"Katya and I walked into the foyer of the Mater Hospital while Ron, Ricardo and Father Renzo parked the car. We had had lunch outdoors at the Fish Market and we wanted to go to the ladies toilet just past reception to wash our hands. As we walked past reception Katya suddenly stopped dead in her tracks and said, "Ah, Jesus." I didn't know what she meant until she turned and walked to a closed door on our left, just short of the toilets. There was no sign on the door, nothing to indicate what it led to. She opened it. It was the Hospital Chapel. She explained that Jesus had called out, "Here I am," as we walked past the door. So we went in, knelt down before the tabernacle and prayed".

Father Renzo, Ricardo and I saw the ladies as we went past and joined them. We all prayed quietly a while. Then we rose and left. In the lift on the way up to the hospital ward Katya broke the silence. "While I was in front of the tabernacle Jesus spoke to me," she said softly. "He said there's a communion host in the pyx in your pocket, Father Renzo. You're to give it to Ron's mother." Father Renzo swears that the pyx was empty before. He is a humble, well-educated and saintly man and I believed him.

During the visit Father Renzo blessed my mother with holy oil and administered to her the host that was not there before. I recalled my exasperated prayer made two days earlier in the same foyer, but might still not have been persuaded that what had happened was miraculous except that my mother amazed everyone by recovering completely and living for another three years. Exactly how generously my prayer had been answered I was still to learn.

CHAPTER 11

SIGNS
FROM GOD

'Australian Story' is a popular documentary series on Australian public television profiling citizens of interest in political, cultural and sporting spheres. Each week a different video portrait is put together on the premise that each subject tells his or her own story. Shortly after our return Mike was the candidate for an upcoming 'Australian Story' feature and in collecting archival and other footage for the production, the producers came across some of the footage I had shot of Mike in Bolivia. It was included in the program when it was broadcast. David Hill, a senior executive from Fox Television in the United States, happened to be in Australia at the time and happened to watch it. The seed was sown. He contacted Mike. Propelled by his intrigue that a journalist of Mike's calibre would independently fund his own research he made an offer. He saw the potential for an investigative piece on the events happening in Bolivia with Mike at the helm. He commissioned a two hour long television special called 'Signs from God'. When completed it was unequivocally remarkable. What was shown had never been seen on television before.

It had seemed from our studies that those people given the 'gift' of the stigmata suffer in the same way Jesus suffered, and also usually suffer at the same time, namely on Fridays or during Easter. With this plausible timetable in mind Mike and myself with a crew of Australian and American film technicians found ourselves in Cochabamba ready and expectant the week before Easter in 1999.

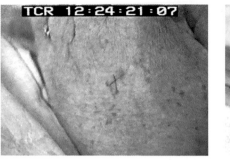
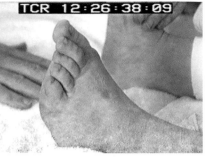
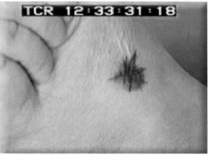
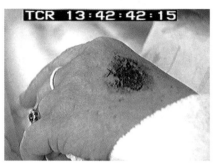
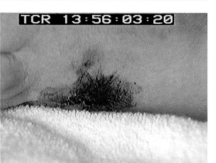
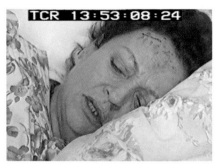
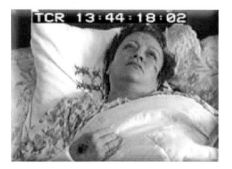
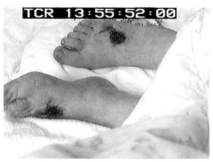

The day before Good Friday, the day before we expected to film the stigmata, we had cameras rolling as Katya received dictation from Jesus. Again, she unhesitatingly wrote the messages she received in her notebook, her face glowing with assuredness and peace, completely divorced from the scrutiny of lenses, lights and microphones. With the same collected demeanor, Katya then stopped without cue, and casually surprised us with a very salient message. She spoke directly to the camera, in close up.

"Jesus says it is not the right time. There will be no stigmata tomorrow. He says it will be in His time and you must learn to trust Him."

Mike and I were crestfallen and by their expressions I had no doubt what the rest of the crew were thinking. She looked completely calm as she said it and I wondered whether she realised just how threatening the statement was to her credibility. She smiled and we left.

The next day there was another message, again imparted to a crew and their cameras.

"It will happen on the day after Corpus Christi and you will be able to come with witnesses and film what happens. I will have wounds which signify the Passion of Christ on my head, my feet and my hands. It will start around noon and end just after 3pm. And it will all heal by the next day. I know this will happen to me, because Jesus said to me it will happen and I believe Him and I trust Him."

So we all packed up and flew thousands of very expensive miles home.

Two months later we were back, ready for what she declared would happen to her on the 4 June 1999, ready for our appointment with God. It was the evening of the 3 June, the feast of Corpus Christi, and we all sat around Katya's kitchen table after finishing a meal. We were enjoying coffee and pastries when Katya became distracted

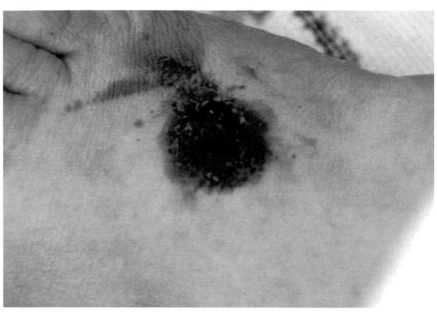

At 1.56 PM

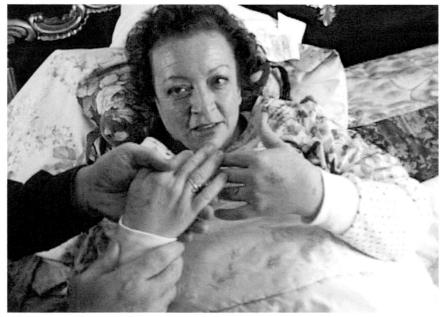

The following morning

and increasingly withdrew from the chatter and laughter. Then she quietly absented herself from the table and we found her a while later on her knees in deep prayer before the little shrine in her room. Words wrought in anguish came haltingly through her sobs as she prayed and wept. She was profoundly distressed.

"It is beginning," said Father Renzo, his own voice faltering. "This is the mirror of Our Lord's agony the night before he was crucified. He was sad unto death because he absorbed and experienced all the sin of every human being, past, present and future. Our sin was his inheritance and his suffering. For this he felt his presence before the Father almost unbearable. In his messages to Katya he says that it was not the scourging, not the nails and the thorns that were most painful. This was the hardest part." He lowered his tender eyes and whispered, "Ah, it is heartbreaking."

The cameras were rolling in the glare of the lights, violating the intimate poignancy of this palpable sorrow. It felt grotesquely and callously invasive, although no one, least of all Katya, insisted that we stop filming.

Katya was in bed, breathing with shuddering rasps of breath when the nine of us arrived the next morning. A distressed Father Renzo sat attentively in a chair alongside. All attempts to make her comfortable with soft pillows seemed in vain. Like vultures around a carcass the television crew trained their cameras on the smooth white skin of her hands as they clutched at the crucifix on her chest. At noon precisely small puncture wounds formed on her forehead, one after another, and as we watched they began to bleed. A swelling began on her left cheek and a dark abrasion appeared as if she had been punched in the face. First her palms, then her feet began to show small scratches in the form of a cross. These then slowly ruptured into open wounds which also began to bleed. Katya was in

The following morning

Mike Willesee co-hosts the Fox Program, "Signs from God"

severe pain, struggling to breathe, mumbling inchoate prayers and contracting in spasms as the hours passed. By 1.30 pm they were already the size of a large coin, maybe 3cm in diameter. As the wounds grew larger and more bloody I couldn't help but think of what it must have been like to see and hear the sound of brutal hammers smashing through the tendons of an innocent man's hands 2000 years ago; I couldn't help but imagine the pain of thorns puncturing the fragile skin of a forehead, soaked in sweat, full of dust and spittle. By 3.00pm I was concerned. Katya was struggling to breathe. She seemed to be dying.

With cameras rolling continuously the spontaneous formation of the wounds was indisputable. Katya was not hypnotized or in any kind of trance. She certainly was not pretending or performing. The wounds were not self-inflicted. They were not externally created by the ingenuity of special effects. From their first spontaneous appearances to their issuing blood, I saw it all. So did everyone else in the room. And so did 20 million viewers of prime time television. The footage was broadcast on the Fox Network as a program called "Signs from God" in July 1999 to massive American and Canadian audiences.

Early the next morning we were greeted by a cheerful bright-eyed Katya, her old self in every way, for no evidence of injury was left on her body. Being in a maelstrom of such supernatural events can be overwhelming. I wasn't sure what was more amazing: the appearance of the gaping, bleeding wounds or the astonishing speed of healing which left not a trace of the trauma of eighteen hours before? I wasn't sure of anything any more except that this was not the work of human beings in their natural understandable world. Katya however was full of confidence and peace. At the end of her ordeal Jesus had spoken to her:
"I have been preparing you for this day because I needed to reach

the world one more time to show the world my suffering through a person like you. Thank you."

What I had seen in the last 24 hours had defied the skeptics, scientists, atheists, nihilists, materialists, rationalists, humanists, existentialists and any other 'ists' left who had any philosophical opposition. A woman had predicted that something pretty bizarre would happen to her body and exactly when it would happen and it did. I had been turned upside down and shaken out. These wounds were suffered by Jesus for a purpose and now they were being repeated by a Bolivian grandmother to remind us of that purpose.

I had researched and filmed some interesting and inexplicable things over the years but the stigmata of Katya was certainly the pinnacle of them all. Nothing could eclipse it. Or so I thought. I should have known better but little did I suspect that there was even more to come.

CHAPTER 12

THE HEART
THAT SUFFERS

The phone call was urgent. Ricardo told me to pack my camera and join him in Argentina. He was onto something but didn't explain. Something to do with a eucharistic host. Something amazing. Within days I was with him in a taxi driving down a hectic Buenos Aires street. It was 5 October 1999 we were on the way to a parish church in the city.

"Some weeks ago," he confided, "Katya spoke to me. She said she had a message from Jesus for me:

'Tell Ricardo I want him to take charge of this case. Through it I want to bring dignity back to my altars.'"

"What did she understand by that message?" I asked

"She said that when Jesus speaks about wanting to bring back dignity to His altars, He is saying that we no longer believe in His Real Presence in the Eucharist, that we have lost respect for Him. We do not venerate Him as we should. She said she imagines that Our Lord has a plan."

"What plan?"

"That we will do tests and show the results in a programme you will make so that this miracle will become known and re-ignite the faith of people. She said people will come to know that Jesus is alive in the Eucharist. And also that Jesus is suffering."

"So what did you do?" I asked, fascinated.

"I couldn't do much without permission, but then I was very fortunate. The Archbishop himself contacted me and asked me to conduct the examination"

"What examination?"

"Wait. You'll see."

We didn't say anything more. We didn't need to. I had the distinct sensation of contentedness, of being in the middle of something orchestrated by forces great and good beyond my own.

We arrived at a brick church in the heart of the commercial district of the city. If anything it seemed incongruously out of place amidst the noise and fumes of unrelenting traffic and trade. Inside we were introduced to Padre Alejandro Pezet, the first of four priests we were to interview, and what he had to say was something almost unthinkable that had occurred three years earlier:

"It was 18 August in 1996," he said, "and I was celebrating the 7pm Mass. When I had just finished distributing Holy Communion to the congregation, a lady came up to me and said she had seen a communion host abandoned in the church and that it was in a candle holder at the base of a crucifix on the right hand side of the church. I gave the ciborium I was holding to a minister of communion and I followed the lady to where I saw the abandoned communion host. It was in a candle holder that we do no use very much. It was very dusty. I picked up the host and took it to the altar with the intention of consuming it. I saw that the host was very dirty and so I asked Emma Fernandez, a minister of communion to put it in a bowl of water and to put it in the tabernacle. She immediately went ahead and did so. I was very much concerned that the host was abandoned by someone who had performed an act of profanation with it." [1]

"And then what happened?" I asked.

"Some days went by and on the morning of Monday the 26 August, I came down to pray in the Blessed Sacrament Chapel of the Church. This was not my normal custom as normally I would pray in the

Chapel of the presbytery. I had taken with me the Vatican newspaper, Osservatore Romano, to read a published letter of John Paul II to the Bishop of Liege, Belgium, which was commemorating the 750th anniversary of the celebration of the Feast of Corpus Christi, which had it's origin in Liege.

Emma Fernandez found me there and said, 'Alejandro, this morning I looked in the tabernacle and noticed something strange.' I got up and went to see. I saw that the host in the tabernacle was becoming red. This had such an impact on me. I felt that what I had seen was something supernatural. This bloodlike substance coming from the host grew in quantity over the following weeks."
"Could someone have placed the red substance in the bowl without your noticing?" I asked.
"The eucharistic Minister and I were the only ones…"
"Emma Fernandez?"
"Yes. We were the only ones with access to the key to the tabernacle. I saw it when it was first put in the tabernacle and locked. After we noticed what had happened I moved the bowl containing the host to the tabernacle in the presbytery. Even if someone could have put something in the bowl before the 26th August without me knowing, you have to ask how that person could gain access to a locked tabernacle in another place and make it change it's characteristics to look like what you see in the photo of 6th September 1996."

He proceeded to show us photographs taken by a professional photographer commissioned by the Archbishop Jorje Bergoglio. [2]

The first were taken on the 26th August and then more were taken twelve days later. I examined the photographs. The first showed a small round glass dish with the round host, still undissolved, and with dark spots surrounded by bright red liquid in the top section. By the 6 September the photos showed that the dark sections had

Padre Alejandro Pezet

Argentine Host transforms (26 August 1996)

Argentine Host continues to transform (6 September 1996)

Dr Castanõn views transformed Argentine Host before taking sample for testing, (5 October 1999)

Dr Castanõn takes sample of Argentine Host for testing (5 October 1999)

Dr Zugibe views Microscopic slide of transformed Argentine Host

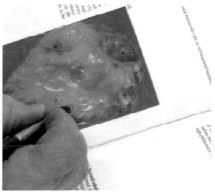

Dr Zugibe shows position of the heart from which the muscle tissue has come

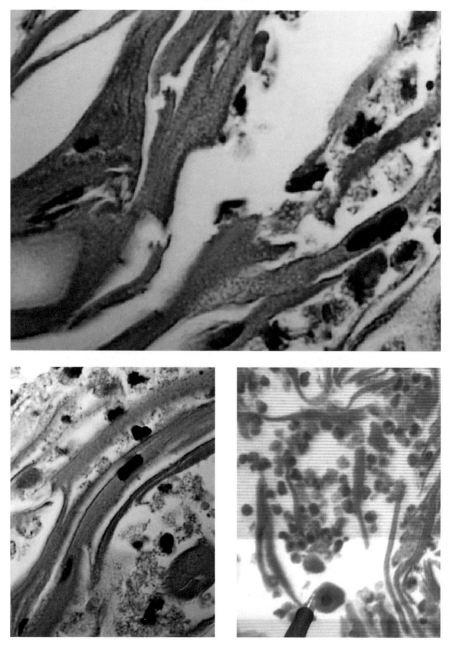

Microscopic sections of sample, revealing inflamed heart tissue

grown and even more red liquid was interspersed with liquid of a ruddy brown colour. The original round outline of the host remained discernible.

Representatives sent by the Archbishop and my rolling camera were witnesses to Ricardo carefully severing a piece of dark 'bloody' material from the host and placing it, together with some of the original water in a test tube. It was sealed and labelled, and again delivered to laboratories for forensic analysis, and again we insisted on a blind test so that the origins of the material remained unknown.

Mike Willesee and I later travelled to New York to film the results of the tests as they were being delivered. The scientist in this case was Dr Frederick Zugibe, a New York heart specialist and forensic pathologist. It was 20 April 2004 and we were in his book-lined office. To him we were simply a television journalist and a lawyer working on an important case which relied on identification of the material preserved on a microscopic slide. Initially he wanted to know what we knew of the origin of the specimen. We held back. He became a little exasperated but then Mike insisted that it would be better for him as well as ourselves if we proceeded with no introduction to the analysis. In hindsight it was ironic that I as the lawyer was doing all the filming and Mike as the television journalist was doing all the talking.

Looking up from a microscope he explained what he was seeing.
"This looks to be of human origin. It is flesh and I can see white blood cells. It is definitely heart tissue from the left ventricle wall, not too far from a valvular area."
"What is the ventricle wall?" I asked.
"It's the part of the heart muscle that makes the heart beat. The left ventricle pumps blood to all parts of the body."
He adjusted his microscope and scrutinized the specimen for a while

before continuing. "This heart muscle has lost its striations and there is the presence of intact white blood cells. The heart muscle is inflamed. There has been recent injury like those that I see in cases where someone has been beaten severely around the chest."

Mike and I looked at each other.

"And the white blood cells, what do they indicate?" Mike asked.

"They indicate injury and inflammation. Well there are a lot of them, all intact. White blood cells can only exist if they are fed by a living body. This sample was alive at the moment it was collected."

This statement created a profound pause and it was a while before Mike could don his professional armour and continue.

"And how long would they remain vital if they were in human tissue that was placed in water."

"Oh," Dr Zugibe replied authoritatively, "they would dissolve within minutes and no longer exist."

As I registered the enormity of what Dr Zugibe had just said I zoomed in very close to his face. He hadn't looked up from the microscope which gave Mike and me free rein to converse in silent facial expressions registering the impact of what we had just heard. We understood each other. I found focus and signalled to Mike.

"What would you say," Mike asked, "if I were to tell you that the source of this sample had been placed in ordinary tap water for a month, then stored for three years in distilled water before a piece was taken and fixed for examination?"

"Absolutely unbelievable. No explanation can be given by science."

Now it was Zugibe's turn to be shocked. He shook his head.

"And what would you say," continued Mike, "if I told you that the source of this specimen was a piece of wheaten bread, a communion host?"

The scientist's eyes widened as he processed information completely alien to his usual territory of mental activity. He seemed to be floundering but then regained a professional composure and constructed a carefully considered response for the camera.

"How or why a communion host could change its character and become living human flesh and blood is outside the ability of science to answer."

He was right. The answers were outside science's ability, but not, it seems, God's. I went back to my books for answers and understanding. I started with the most common, most famous book in the world.

(1)
By placing the abandoned host in water, Padre Alejandro was complying with a procedure outlined by the Church. Since every particle of the consecrated bread and wine is accepted as sacred, as being God truly present, it then follows that every part must be solemnly consumed. If this is not possible, for instance if small crumbs remain on the altar cloths, or drops remain in the chalices or as in this case the host is too soiled, then these are dissolved into the water in which they are washed and laundered. This water is then poured into a special sink called a sacrarium which leads to consecrated ground in the Church precinct.

(2)
On 23 September 2005, the Associated Press published unauthorised diary excerpts from one of the 115 Cardinals who entered the conclave to elect a new Pope. The diarist's name was not revealed. Cardinal Joseph Ratzinger was elected and became Pope Benedict XVI. What the diary reveals is that Cardinal Jorge Bergoglio, a Jesuit, was Ratzinger's only challenger and was successively in second place throughout the voting.

CHAPTER 13

THE REAL PRESENCE OF JESUS CHRIST

"On the night before he was betrayed, while at supper with his disciples Jesus took bread, said the blessing, broke the bread and gave it to His disciples saying, *"Take this, all of you and eat it. This is My Body which will be given up for you."* In the same way He took the cup filled with wine. He gave thanks and giving the cup to His disciples said, *"Take this all of you and drink from it. This is the cup of my blood, the blood of the new and everlasting covenant. It will be shed for you and for all so that sins may be forgiven. Do this in memory of me."* These are the words of consecration at Mass which are taken from Luke 22:17-20 and Matthew 26:26-29

The Catholic Church teaches and believes that at the consecration of the bread and wine during the Mass it becomes 'truly, really and substantially the Body and Blood, Soul and Divinity of our Lord Jesus Christ.' The bread and wine still look the same but through a mysterious process called transubstantiation the substance of the bread and wine is changed into a truly present Jesus, as present as if he were actually standing there in person. This is the Blessed Eucharist.

This belief in the Sacrament of the Holy Eucharist is one of the central and most important teachings in the Church and has been since it's very beginning. It is a belief of immense and magnificent ramifications. It means that the very same Creator, the Creator of the entire universe, the same God who will judge us to determine our eligibility to enter His promised eternal kingdom, the God who is Love itself, humbles Himself to come to His creatures as beneficial spiritual food in the communion host. It not only bestows grace but is the source of Grace itself. Pope John Paul II described it as, "God's answer to the deepest longings of the human heart."

The most powerful discourse on the Holy Eucharist comes straight from St John's Gospel. Chapter 6 made for riveting reading after what I had filmed in Argentina and New York. In it Jesus repeats four times the injunction to eat his flesh. The fact of the Holy Eucharist is difficult, probably impossible, to fully understand. It is 'a hard saying; who can listen to it?' they said two thousand years ago. Today it's just as hard. In those days many loyal followers simply couldn't accept on faith that when Jesus said they were to eat his body and drink his blood, he meant exactly that. It contradicted the Mosaic prohibition against the consumption of blood. The concept was intolerable and scandalous. They left and no longer followed him. He lost most of his longtime and closest disciples over this declaration. Surely, if it was a simple misunderstanding he wouldn't have allowed such a catastrophe, particularly in the light of his past habit of correcting his listeners when they took something he said the wrong way. [1]

Jesus often used parables to tell of spiritual truths, and he helped his listeners interpret their meaning if they had difficulty. He also used words literally or figuratively. When he spoke figuratively but was taken literally he usually corrected the misunderstanding of his listeners immediately. When he spoke literally and was correctly understood but his listeners refused to accept what he said he reasserted his literal meaning again even more forcibly, as he does in this chapter.

The messages of Katya were no different and very beautiful.

"When you contemplate the sacred Host you see a round white shape, seemingly bearing no other glory than being raised by the hand of a priest. Indeed such is the ceremony of the Altar, the candles, the flowers, the prayers and the sighs of My faithful. I welcome it with joy because your praises are reversed: you profess your faith although you cannot notice any sign of My Glory when you look at the whiteness of the Host."

My children, look at Me and sigh for Me, because your looks, your sighs and your heartbeats never escape Me. I can see all of you distinctly. I see you from that whitest and purest Host although you cannot detect Me. Oh, I am so pleased by your love although I am concealed in the greatest sacrament that I have left for mankind! If I could be seen it would be easy to love Me, I know. Although you have not seen Me you have believed. You must believe that when you look at the sacred Host you are indeed beholding Jesus Himself who now speaks to you. And He always speaks to the Father on your behalf, and praises you in Heaven for your faith of today and shall praise you tomorrow when you are with Me up here. [(2)]

If I should let myself be seen openly, I advise you that there would not be enough Eucharistic vessels nor hosts to nourish the enormous crowds that would come to Me. Come forth then with faith to nourish yourselves from Me because there is no greater honour than to receive Holy Communion, that is to say, to unite with My humanity and My divinity. Oh, yes, it is an honour and it should always be your wish to nourish yourselves from Me, because I am the food for your souls, I am the Truth for your minds, I am the fire that warms all hearts and ignites all souls. My beloved, come without fear, come to Me." [(3)]

For men of faith, My Eucharistic form is a gateway to Bethlehem where they adore me, like angels, the shepherds and the Magi. For those enlightened with the brilliance of the faith, in each altar where sacrifice is elevated, a new Calvary is raised and with feelings of profound adoration, those words are repeated; 'Truly, here is the Son of God.

As men receive communion they get to know me more intimately and listen from the depths of their hearts to my supreme teachings. I, being the teacher, increase the light in the minds of those who receive me, so that they can penetrate more into the profundity of my doctrine......Happy are My Apostles, who, after their first communion at the Cenacle said: now we understand everything you tell us... Happy doubting Thomas, who touching My wounds burst forth into an intense act of faith and love. Happy are the disciples of Emmaus, who recognised the pilgrim as the One who lit their hearts... Happy are the poor and ignorant according to the world, who through continual contact with Me have learned celestial knowledge, the knowledge which communicates faith, strengthened by the celestial banquet. These privileged beings not only have faith, but live justly, acquiescing in practice to my orders. Blessed are they! More blessed still are those whose faith in My Sacrament has been rewarded with miracles." [4]

The writings shed light on the evident trauma in the Argentine Eucharistic miracle that Dr Zugibe detected.

"I offered Myself to fulfill the work of redeeming the world. Ah what a moment it was when I felt all those torments come over Me, the torments I was to suffer in My Passion, the slander, the insults, the scourging, the kicks, the Crown of Thorns, the Cross.... All that passed before my eyes at the same time that an intense pain hurt My Heart; the offences, the sins, and the abominations that would be committed in the passing of time.... This heart of Mine suffers because each day the number of sins that are committed is greater; greater each time are the sufferings that afflict it filling it with

bitterness. You do not know nor could you imagine the number of sins, blasphemies, and sacrileges, the lukewarmness and indifference of so many souls that call themselves kind and their compassion is only a cover for hypocrisy. My Heart is a burning furnace passionate with Love for the salvation of souls. It bleeds and suffers. Day after day men go on accumulating iniquities for their own damnation. This is my torment!" [5]

The Church, in no uncertain terms, expresses that the Eucharist is the source and summit of the faith. Pope Benedict XVI says it is 'the heart of Christian life and the source of the evangelising mission of the Church... (it) cannot but be the permanent centre and the source of the petrine service entrusted to me.' And yet it is today misunderstood or ignored or disregarded by many within the Catholic Church itself. Surveys in the United States show that only 30% of Catholics believe in the Real Presence. In Australia it is even worse with only 27% of final year students in Catholic Universities believing in the Real Presence, (Australian Catholic magazine, *AD2000*). Only 5% of students graduating from Catholic schools in Australia practise their faith as young adults. The central core teaching of the Church is, for an overwhelming majority, not understood at best, or completely rejected at worst. Most it seems have what is basically a Protestant belief concerning the Eucharist: that Jesus was speaking metaphorically or symbolically when he said that he would give us His Body to eat and His blood to drink.

It was dawning on me exactly how powerful and how generous was the gift to my mother and to my brother Vince. God had given them Himself in response to my prayers; to my mother in a miraculous host that appeared out of nowhere and which graced her with a completely unforeseen recovery; to Vince as a final act of salvation. I saw it as a testimonial to the depth of Christ's love and mercy.

St Thomas Aquinas, the great academic and theologian of the Church, took on the whole weight of the history of philosophy and in its own terms and according to its own methodologies of logic produced a huge body of work in his *'Summa Theologicae.'* Here, somewhat simplified, is what he has to say about the Eucharist:

He instituted this sacrament at the Last Supper because He knew that the last words and actions of men who are about to leave this world are more likely to be remembered with love and devotion than any other words or actions. The Eucharist was, as it were, His last will and testament to the human race. Shortly before His death, resurrection and ascension into heaven, He left men His Body and Blood as food for their souls. It was the most precious gift He had to leave us, because the Eucharist is Christ Himself, the Author and Dispenser of God's grace.

(1) Consider how he explains His meaning when misunderstood in these passages.
    Example 1: Matthew 16:5 and verses 11-12
    Example 2: John 11:11 and verse 14
    Example 3: John 3:3 and 4
    Example 4: John 8:56 and 57
(2) The Crusade of Mercy (24)
(3) The Crusade of Mercy (141)
(4) The Door to Heaven (22)
(5) The Crusade of Love (81)

CHAPTER 14

CENTURIES OF STORIES

By August 2001 Mike Willesee and I were almost finished making a documentary on the Eucharist. In it we were presenting the traditional teaching of the Church, our findings in Argentina and what we discovered through further research. There had been many other reported instances of Eucharistic miracles in the history of the Catholic Church. The most celebrated was that of the miracle of Lanciano in Italy at the beginning of the 9th century. It had similarities to the modern Buenos Aires case.

The story is told of a priest of the order of St Basil who had sincere doubts about the Body and Blood of Christ being really and substantially present in the host and chalice. Nevertheless he went through the motions of his priestly functions at Mass without believing that any transubstantiation could possibly take place. At the moment of consecration, in the presence of many witnesses, the bread turned to flesh and the wine to blood. The blood in the chalice coagulated into five separate clots of unequal size. Nearly eight hundred years later, on 17 February 1574, by the authority of Archbishop Rodriguez, the five separate clots of coagulated blood were weighed and although of varying sizes, each one of a different size respectively equaled the weight of the five clots taken together. The Archbishop declared that the Lord wanted to show in this way what the Holy Church teaches; that Christ is totally present in the smallest fragment of the consecrated host and in the smallest drop of consecrated wine.

So we took ourselves and our cameras to Lanciano where this miraculous flesh and blood is still on display in glass vials in the Church of St Francis. The Conventual Friars Minor, to whom is entrusted the care of the church in which the miracle occurred, wished to verify the authenticity of the miracle for modern times. Rome granted its authorisation and so a group of experts were invited to examine the Flesh and coagulated Blood. Between November 1970 and March 1971, laboratory tests were conducted by Professor Edoardo Linoli, Professor in Anatomy and Pathological Histology and in Chemistry and Clinical Microscopy and Professor Ruggero Bertoli from the University of Sienna.

In 2001 Ricardo, Mike and I managed to locate the elderly and rather subdued Professor Linoli. During an interview he discussed his findings with us. Although they were conducted thirty years earlier, Linoli explained them with manifest enthusiasm and excitement as if his discoveries had been made that very same day. This is what he had to say:

1. The substances at issue are truly flesh and blood.
2. The flesh and blood are from a human source.
3. The flesh is constituted in sections of the myocardium, the endocardium, the vagus nerve and also the left ventricle of a human heart.
4. The flesh is a 'heart', complete in its essential structure.
5. The flesh and blood (bread and wine) are of the same blood type, AB. (relatively rare and confined to the geography of the Mediterranean)
6. On microscopic inspection the blood contained proteins in the same normal proportions as are found in the sero-proteic make-up of fresh blood. It corresponded with human blood taken from a man's body that very same day.

7. No traces were found anywhere of a permeation of the organic tissue by any substance designed to preserve them.
8. No sign, not even of incipient corruption, degradation or decomposition, was observed, although the relics have been exposed for centuries to the action of physical, atmospheric, and biological agents.

To a question Mike posed about how he felt when he first saw the results of the tests, he responded without hesitation, "Oh I felt as if I was floating 35 centimetres above the ground!" I had to smile. Science has given us its results, but science cannot furnish any explanation.

In Orvieto, again in Italy, this time in the 13th century, another priest had doubts as he raised the host in consecration. At that moment it began to bleed, dripping onto his hands and onto the altar cloth in full view of an amazed congregation. It was the catalyst for the Pope at the time, Pope Urban IV, to commission from St Thomas Aquinas the liturgy for the new feast he was to institute, the feast of Corpus Christi, the feast of the Body of Christ.[1] That same altar cloth, stained with blood, still exists today and, as we captured on film, is reverently paraded through the streets of Orvieto every year on the feast of Corpus Christi. It made for quite a spectacular scene. The ceremonial pageantry, reverence and pride of the people of Orvieto for the historic part their town played in the unfolding mystery of the Eucharist were all quite stirring.

When it was finally edited I was really pleased with the documentary. It underlined, for what I imagined would be a largely Catholic audience, that the keystone of their faith remains as true as ever and should be treasured for the gift that it is. These revelations would be incentives, I hoped, to an acceptance of the true miracle within reach of them all: Christ risen and present in the Holy

Professor Odoardo Linoli

*Painting of Orvieto miracle occurring
(Vatican Museum)*

*Pope Urban IV views miracle
(tapestry in Orvieto)*

*The bloodstained cloth carried in
procession in Orvieto, Italy*

Close up of the Eucharistic miracle

*Reliquary containing
Eucharistic Miracle of
Lanciano*

Eucharist. The audience's response to the film, which was to be as miraculous as the subject matter, had to wait though, for it would be another year before we launched the film. In the mean time I turned my attention to my family. My mother was sick.

(1)
A feast is declared by the Church as an annual day of public celebration in honour of a sacred attribute, event or holy person such as a saint

CHAPTER 15

MY MOTHER
AND OUR MOTHER

Bertha turned 89 and celebrated her birthday in hospital. It was three years since she had consumed the host that appeared out of thin air in answer to my prayer, three years since we had envisaged her to be within days of death. This time she was in for some tests. Children and grandchildren gathered round her bedside as the birthday gifts were admired. One of them, from her grandchild, was a little booklet on the Rosary, which caused Bertha's face to light up and reach over to the top drawer of the hospital locker. From it she retrieved a worn and dog-eared version of the same publication. This one was a 1953 edition, as tired and frail as my mother, with thin stained pages held together with paper clips and cellotape. It was the same one she'd used every day for over fifty years when she prayed the meditations of the Rosary.

With all the medical examinations completed she returned home to her retirement unit. I phoned her a week later.
"Hi Mum, how are you?"
"I am OK."
"Good, that's good to hear. I'm coming to see you this morning. I will take you to the doctor to pick up your X-Rays and then maybe we can have lunch together somewhere."
"Don't come down too early because there's a priest coming to see me."
"What priest?"
"Oh I don't know him. Someone Olga saw at Mass on Sunday

Bertha's grand-daughter,
Ron's daughter, Katrina

NIHIL OBSTAT:
JOHN M. FEARNS, S.T.D.
Censor Librorum

IMPRIMATUR:
† FRANCIS CARDINAL SPELLMAN, D.D.
Archbishop of New York

Feast of the Assumption
August 15, 1953

When you say the Rosary
say "Whatever you ask through the
Rosary shall be granted."
Promise of Our Lady to St. Dominic

Oh my Jesus forgive
us our sins, save us
from the fires of Hell
i lead all souls to
heaven, especially those

Copyright 1953
Catholic Book Publishing Co., N. Y.
United States and Canada
Printed and Bound in U.S.A.

in most of need.

Preface

I HOPE that this beautiful little
book will be your guide to a
richer and more intimate understanding of the Holy Rosary.

Keep it handy in your home and
in your pocket or purse, because it
is an inspiration to loving meditation
on the Mysteries of Our Lord Jesus
as you address Our Blessed Lady in
petition and thanksgiving.

May Jesus and Mary bless all who
use it with tender and personal devotion.

Father Patrick Peyton, C.S.C.

-5-

Bertha's Rosary Prayer Book

morning. She said he would be here at 10.30 this morning." Olga Keller lived in the same retirement village as Bertha.

"Okay well I'll see you then about noon."

"Okay Ronny. Bye."

"Bye Ma. See you later."

When I did see my mother just a few hours later I was struck by how different she had sounded on the phone such a short while before. She was distinctly weaker and had deteriorated alarmingly. I stayed and watched as she progressively declined losing control of her limbs and then her co-ordination. She couldn't guide a spoon to her mouth to feed herself. Before long she became unable to move. The next morning she was taken to hospital suffering intense pain from the spreading cancer in her body. Hefty doses of morphine gave her body some respite but she slipped into semi-consciousness. Four days later I found myself with my brother at her bedside, but she didn't show any signs of consciousness. It was disturbing that she didn't recognise us at all. Every breath she took was difficult. This time our mother was surely dying.

We left together at about 4pm, took the lift down to the ground floor to find a cup of coffee. I kept looking at my watch, not wanting to be away too long, and so I knew it was 4.30 when we encountered my cousin, Louise and her husband in the corridor. They had just left her bedside. More and more family members arrived to share the grave situation. We greeted each other in an atmosphere made tense by the momentous event so clearly close by. I checked the time again. 5.30 pm. Sadness and solemnity are not good companions with conversation. Words don't come easily in the face of death. But prayers do.

"Let's say the 'Hail Mary'" I suggested. I was thinking of her battered old prayer book which contained the deepest sighs and supplications of the ebbing life before me. I wanted to speak for her.

Bertha shows her prayer book

Michaelangelo's Pieta

"If Mum could she would have liked to say this prayer herself now."
And so, for the first time I can remember, my brothers and I joined
in intoning the Rosary prayer our mother had prayed every day.

"Hail Mary, full of grace.
The Lord is with thee
Blessed art thou among women
And blessed is the fruit of thy womb, Jesus.
Holy Mary, mother of God,
Pray for us sinners now and at the hour of our death
Amen."

Everyone left and only Katrina, my daughter, and I remained.
I looked at my watch again. It was 6.15 and dark.
"Dad," she said softly, "while there's no-one else here, I mean I was
a bit shy in case the others didn't want to… I mean… I'd really like
to say this prayer with you." She gestured towards the small book in
her hands. "It's a prayer that Jesus gave to Sister Faustina."
"Faustina?"
"She was a nun from Poland in the 1930's and she's a saint now.
In fact she was canonized a few months ago. Anyway Jesus said,"
and she read from her booklet, " *If this prayer is said in the company
of a dying person, I promise My Divine Mercy and the graces for
that person to enter heaven.*"

Before me was a beautiful scene, and I willed it to mould a lasting
memory. With tears in her eyes was my daughter beseeching her God,
the God my mother was about to meet, for His mercy. Katrina's depth
of faith was evident and considerable. She had no doubt that He would
honour His promise. My mother lay motionless, her granddaughter
prayed quietly as she wept. It was impossible for a compassionate
heavenly Father not to be moved if a merely mortal one was.

Katrina persevered through the agonizing distractions of my mother's laboured breathing. Then all of a sudden, my mother opened her eyes for the first time in days, turned to Katrina, and smiled a smile clear and bright and full of joy.

"Nonna, Nonna," Katrina cried out excitedly. She stood up from her chair and leaned over to kiss her grandmother, "Nonna, I love you." Bertha then slowly turned her head back and returned to that place out of our reach from whence she'd emerged to bestow a smile. She was breathing easily and regularly now and Katrina returned to finish her prayer: *"Holy God, holy mighty one holy immortal one, have mercy on us and on the whole world."* Katrina pronounced the final *"Amen"* and in perfect synchronicity my mother expired her last breath.

It was over. I looked at my watch. It was 6.26 pm. Nothing is quite as still as the air in a room where a person has just died.

CHAPTER 16

POST
MORTEM

This is not a post mortem in any medical or legal sense. It is a series of discoveries I made after my mother's death, discoveries related to prayer and it's power in life and death.

There is a tradition in the Catholic Church that attributes the origin of the Rosary to the 13th century when the Virgin Mary appeared to St Dominic and promised certain graces to all those who have a devotion to it. One of them was that no-one who perseveres in the saying of the Rosary will die without receiving the sacraments of the dying. Everyone who says these prayers is promised the chance of dying at peace having made a full confession, being absolved of their sins, and taking communion. This essentially means having access to a priest who alone can administer the rites.

I spoke to my mother's friend from the retirement village, Olga, and told her that Bertha had died. She offered condolences and then spoke at length.

"I saw your mother when my granddaughter was in the same hospital, when she was having some tests. I used to just poke my head in and say hello. And then when she came home I saw her a couple of times. She showed me her Rosary prayer book and the prayers she said. Something, I don't know what, made me ask her, 'Bertha, do you want to see a priest?' She said straight away, 'Yes. Yes I would.' It's funny, you know, it's not something I would normally do, but somehow something just pushed me to ask. I didn't really know how to go about it, so I rang someone in the parish. I spoke to Father Crawford and he said he was pretty sure he could come on Tuesday morning. He had to check his appointment book.

So he came up on the Tuesday. I went with him to your mother's unit. He said to me, 'If she wants to say confession you will have to leave.' The priest talked and joked with her for a while. Then he asked her about confession. She said, 'Yes, but to you, here, not down at the Church.' And so I went outside for a while and when I came back he gave her the rest of the Sacraments. I saw him out and I went back to her for a while but then I had to leave for an appointment. The next thing I hear she's in hospital."

When Olga arranged for a priest to see my mother, there was no reason for her to believe that Tuesday would be the last day Bertha would spend at home before leaving for the hospital never to return. Thanks to Olga's responding to 'something (that) prompted me to ask,' my mother received the Sacrament of the dying a mere hour or two before she was to lose her physical and mental independence at the end of a life of nearly 90 years.

When I spoke to Father Crawford he said, "When I saw her it was about 10.30. She seemed fine. She asked for, and received the Sacraments." I knew this already, but I had to follow up and confirm what Olga had told me. I like being sure of things.

Calling family members with the news of my mother's death meant calling my cousin Louise. I remembered bumping into her and Tony, her husband, at the hospital lift as they were leaving, just before the end.
"When did she die?" she asked.
"Not too long after you left." I answered.

"I knew it would not be long when I saw her. So when did you say she died."

"Oh, a couple of hours later?"

"No, I mean what time did she die?"

"6.26." I was perplexed by her fixation on the detail of the time of death. What difference did it make?

"Are you sure?" she asked, still not satisfied.

"Yes. It was exactly 6.26pm"

"And Tony and I left just before 4.30. So that makes it exactly two hours after we left. Praise be to God. It's just marvellous."

She was still going on about the time and I didn't understand.

"What do you mean, 'marvellous'?"

"Well, Ronny it's a long story. But it really means that God is so very good keeping His promises."

What promises?"

"The promises He makes to those who pray."

"What are you talking about, Louise?"

"You see I don't know if you realise that I became very close to your mother and I spent a lot of time with her. She would listen and understand when I had something to whinge about and I would do the same for her. We had a wonderful understanding of each other. When she was in hospital in a lot of pain with this dreaded cancer, she knew she wouldn't get better this time, the doctor's were saying it, and she told me she wasn't scared of dying, only scared of the pain. She showed me the Pieta prayer book Gabi had given her and we prayed from it together. You know, of course that she wouldn't miss saying the Rosary every day. Anyway I saw one of those Pieta prayer books at Church and I bought one and I took it with me when Tony and I went to the hospital that last time. We arrived at 4pm, but the nurses were busy attending to Aunty Bertha and so we waited in the TV room until 4.15 when they let us in to see her."

It dawned on me that I wasn't the only one watching the clock that Sunday. It must be a family trait.

"Aunty Bertha was lying there breathing very heavily. She was assisted with a lot of medical equipment. But she looked very beautiful Ronny; peaceful in her clean white night gown with the long sleeves covering her bruised arms."

Louise paused then and sighed. "But I knew. Somehow we just know these things. I knew she was not returning so I said to her that it was all right to leave us and that the others in the next world were all waiting for her. I kissed her and then I took out my Pieta prayer book and turned to the prayers for the dying. I began reading the special prayer, 'Consecration of the last two hours of life to the Holy Mother of God', and I read it to her. I then kissed her goodbye and left."

"And precisely two hours later she died."

"Exactly. Exactly. Now Ron do you see what I mean?"

Later I sought out Gabrielle's copy of the Pieta. On its cover was a photograph of Michelangelo's exquisitely beautiful sculpture with the lifeless marble corpse of Jesus in his mother's arms. I couldn't take my eyes off it. She was with him to the very end, a tender symbol of what Catholics understand her maternal role to be, and what my mother certainly believed. Then I read the prayer that my cousin prayed:

> 'Prostrated at thy feet and humiliated by my sins, but full of confidence in thee, O Mary, I beg thee to accept the petition my heart is going to make. It is for my last moments. Dear Mother, I wish to request thy protection and Maternal love so that in the decisive instant thou wilt do all thy love can suggest on my behalf. To thee, O mother of my soul, I consecrate the last two hours of my life. Come to my side and receive my last breath. I put my trust in thee, my Mother.'

I remembered my brothers and I praying at our mother's deathbed and had two thoughts: the time, around 5.30 pm and the last line of our prayer, 'Pray for us sinners, now and at the hour of our death'.

In response to the news of my mother's death I received a reply of condolence from Katya, and an assurance from a message she received from Jesus. My mother, he said, had been received into the arms of his mother. The Pieta booklet lay before me and the image on its cover burned into my consciousness. My mother's soul, I knew, was not alone in passing on to the next phase of its existence and I was filled with profound peace and joy at the realization.

The mind-picture I still cherish is that of the tiny form of my dying mother and my beautiful daughter ardently praying at her side. Only her fingers counting rosary beads and her lips moved. Otherwise the scene was quite still. The words too, repeated over and over like a rhythm of soft rain, form a soundtrack to the image:

> For the sake of His sorrowful Passion have mercy on us and on the whole world.
> For the sake of His sorrowful Passion have mercy on us and on the whole world
> For the sake of His sorrowful Passion have mercy on us and on the whole world.

"It was the first death I ever witnessed, and it was a most beautiful experience. I felt completely at peace," reflected Katrina.

Reading the diary of Sister Faustina, this nun I first learned about in my mother's dying moments, I uncovered the promise Katrina had remembered and acted upon. For both herself and my mother, together in a final moment, was truly a peace beyond all human understanding.

Saint Faustina was a nun who had lived and died in Poland in 1938. In 1931 she mystically experienced seeing Jesus and hearing His voice. Under obedience to her spiritual director she recorded these in a fascinating diary. She writes insistently of God's mercy as immensely greater than we can ever imagine, that mercy is 'love's second name'. (Her role in this story and the message she relayed to the world is significant enough to warrant its own chapter later on.)

This is the promise given by Jesus regarding the praying of the Chaplet of Divine Mercy. Little wonder Katrina felt compelled to say it beside her dying grandmother. It's an unbelievably generous gift.

> *Say unceasingly the chaplet I have taught you. Whoever will recite it will receive great mercy at the hour of death.* [1]

> *When they say this chaplet in the presence of the dying, I will stand between my Father and the dying person, not as a just Judge but as the merciful Saviour.* [2]

I uncovered an account written by Sister Faustina chronicling the first time she ever said the chaplet at the bedside of a dying person:

> 'The following afternoon when I entered the ward, I saw someone dying, and learned the agony had started during the night…. Just then, I heard a voice in my soul, *'Say the chaplet which I taught you'*. I ran to fetch my rosary and knelt down beside the dying person and, with all the ardour of my soul, I began to say the chaplet. Suddenly the dying person opened her eyes and looked at me. I had not finished the entire chaplet when she died, with extraordinary peace. I fervently asked the Lord to fulfill the promise He had given me for the recitation of the chaplet. The Lord gave me to know that the soul had been granted the grace He had promised.' [3]

I saw my mother's dying moments resonating in this description, her suddenly opening her eyes and falling back into a sublime peace and

Katrina declaring confidently, "It took away any fear of death I might have had before that."

(1) Diary of Sister Faustina (205)
(2) Diary of Sister Faustina (1541)
(3) Diary of Sister Faustina (810)

CHAPTER 17

BLIND
MEN SEE

Adelaide was warm on the summer evening on the 19 November 2003 and the Dom Polski Centre was packed with people who'd come for the launch of the documentary Mike and I had made. It was called, 'The Eucharist; In Communion with Me.' It presented the traditional teachings of the Church about the Real Presence and included material on the Eucharistic miracles of Argentina, Lanciano and Orvieto. As we had done in previous presentations we showed the film and then invited questions or comments from the floor. There were the usual ones like why more wasn't said about Eucharistic miracles, and how can we get this on television and into our schools, and this is so completely different from what was taught at school. Then an old man tapping a white cane made his way haltingly to the microphone.

"My name is Harold O'Shea," he said. "I am 84 years old and basically you could say I am blind. But tonight I came along to hear Mike Willesee and when the film started…," and he swallowed, breathed deeply and continued with emotional difficulty, "and….and ..tonight I saw. Perfectly, clearly, the whole film. I watched it right through and then lost it on the credits."
There was a hush of silence in the hall. Mike and I were too astonished to say anything. Harold spoke first. "When it started I said, 'Lord please let me see this film because I know it's going to be special. And He did. I saw the lovely little girl receiving communion on her tongue and her bright pure eyes as she looked up

at the priest and said 'Amen' and I saw everything in focus… just perfectly right to the end."

"And now?" Mike asked.

"Now it's back to the way it was before. It's …. It's.." Harold was overcome with raw feeling and couldn't continue. He sat down.

All of this took me very much by surprise. I knew that the old man believed that something incredible had happened to him. He was an unassuming character and seemed visibly shaken by his recent experience. I was predisposed to believing him but I held myself back from expressing solidarity with his claim until I could further explore the matter. Mike too was full of excitement but remained serene in his polished professional way. After all we still had an audience before us with a few raised arms calling for our attention. The master of ceremonies concluded the evening and we began packing up. Mike was the focus of attention for a long queue of people seeking autographs. One woman wouldn't wait in line. She edged in sideways and said, "It happened to my friend too."

"Excuse me?" Mike asked.

"She saw it."

"I'm sorry," he said. "Who saw what?" and noticed how anxious she was.

"My friend, Pauline, sitting next to me, she saw the film too. I just thought I must let you know."

"I'm glad. And did she enjoy it?"

"Very."

"That's good to hear."

"No, no, I mean she saw it. Like that other man." She was becoming nervous as she struggled to make herself understood. "She's blind you see. Yes. It's true. Legally blind. She didn't say anything. She didn't want others to think she was just climbing on the bandwagon, you know, because of you being here and all."

"Where is she?" he looked around.

"She's already left. She's very shy. But she told me she saw the whole thing and she said it in a very strange way. And so I quizzed her and she must have seen it. Must have. Anyway I just thought I'd let you know."

"Yes, thank you, thank you very much." For a moment he was distracted by a murmur of dissension from the queue. She had pushed in. So he decided to finish with the signing of autographs and then find her and, better still, find her blind friend.

But she had vanished. He walked outside to see if he could catch up with her but she was nowhere to be seen.

About two weeks later Mike and I flew back to Adelaide, this time with camera gear to interview Harold and hopefully also the mystery woman, Pauline. Attempts to locate her by Paul Russell, who had so efficiently organized the initial screening, were in vain so a notice was published in the local Catholic newspaper asking for help. So far we'd had no luck but were determined to interview Harold anyway.

I had a particular angle to explore which I had pretty much kept to myself. It seemed so secondary to the obvious fascination of speaking to a blind man who claimed to have seen a video that I didn't want to distract from the work at hand. A brief interlude of perfect vision divinely endowed for the purpose of watching a video was more than enough to focus on. Yet it was something Harold said the night of his 'mini-miracle', as he called it, that resonated in me and wouldn't let up. It was that he specifically mentioned one shot amongst thousands: the shot of the child receiving her first holy communion; the look of wonderment on her face.

I too had been struck by it and I so clearly remember the exhilaration I myself experienced during the actual filming. It was a powerful sensation of a kind I had never had before or have experienced since. Father Aliprandi, the same priest who walked into my office all those years ago and turned my life around, had graciously allowed me to record children receiving their first Holy Communion. It was hard work. I had been filming all morning and was well placed to capture the children's faces as they received the host from the priest. One by one they stepped into frame. Then a little girl entered my viewfinder and I had an unforgettable and conscious sense of this shot being exceptional. In fact, I deliberately and confidently judged it to be perfect. I was filled with an unusual euphoria at that moment and everything just fell effortlessly in place: the lighting, the focus, the rhythm, the framing, all the technical parameters were somehow right. But it was the look on her innocent face, her reverence and purity which made it so sublimely beautiful. In six seconds I felt I had encapsulated the meaning of the entire film.

It was a rare experience for me to feel this way about a shot and I couldn't quite verbalise how special that moment was. And now, more than a year later I had encountered a man who shared my enthusiasm for what I had seen. And that man was blind.

At his home we realised exactly how blind he was when he showed us the special magnification technology he used to read. A text would be scanned and then appear on a monitor radically magnified so that a single letter of the alphabet moved across the average sized monitor one at a time, occupying the height and width of the entire screen. Little wonder he claims not to have seen the choir which was on stage as he made his way to the microphone that incredible night. We had a closer look at the monocular which he fixed on a tripod in front of his television set and which provided magnification which allowed him to discern a vague outline of the broadcast image. It was the same monocle that he had tried, then abandoned, that night in Adelaide.

"I have macular degeneration, and so I can only slightly see very blurred edges of objects. Anyway I saw the whole film in perfect focus, completely miraculously." Harold then listed detail after detail of the images in the film which left us in no doubt that he had seen the film. He described scenes that were accompanied solely by a music score and whose content would have been undetectable save via the direct act of visual perception. He kept referring to the image of the little child receiving communion which so moved and amazed him and me. Perhaps most touching were his constant references to his delight at having seen the film itself, rather than the actual surprise of regaining his sight. It was the film which he kept referring to in terms of wonder. There was not a trace of bitterness in his being as blind as before his short and miraculous experience.

"And what did your doctor have to say?"

"Entirely shocked at my claim. Said it was not possible, you know, medically speaking… I was so overjoyed by the whole thing, and I don't know whether I would have been more happy if I had my sight returned than I was to have had just that 35 minutes of vision." He bought four copies and shared them with friends – a blind man enthusiastically championing something he 'saw' was simply amazing to me.

John Kelly was at the screening and he said: "Before the presentation began, I noticed an elderly gentleman enter and take a seat across the aisle from me, some four rows in front. He caught my attention because of the red and white stick in his possession. I took no notice of the gentleman until the commencement of the video, and then, because he was directly in my line of sight, I saw him in semi-silhouette. He seemed to initially use some sort of viewing instrument, held as one would hold opera glasses. Not long after the screening began, the gentleman abandoned the use of the instrument. I attended no more to him, finding myself more intent on the video itself, and only adverted again to the gentleman when he later left his seat to approach the microphone and gave the account of what he experienced, displaying to the audience what appeared to be the same viewing instrument. After the gentleman had spoken (he was evidently moved) I remarked to my mother who was seated next to me, 'We might just have witnessed a miracle!' "

In my view the testimony of Harold was strong and genuine. I agreed with his son John whose assessment of his father was one of unbounded admiration and respect.

"Some people have fathers and some people have special fathers. He is a special father. What he says is right to the letter. If he says it, it is one hundred percent true. I have absolutely no doubt. Not one bit. It's true. All of it."

We returned well satisfied to Paul Russell's office so that we could pack up and go home. A woman there recognized Mike.

"Hallo, Mike," she said introducing herself. "It's such a pleasure to meet you. The whole parish has been really excited by the happenings related to your movie. "

"Yes," he said, "it's all been quite astonishing."

"So what are you doing back here?"

He pointed to all the gear and said, "We've been filming Harold, the blind man that saw the film, and he's been explaining exactly what happened."

"Oh yes, I heard all about it. Why don't you interview Pauline?"

"Pauline?"

"My friend, Pauline Grzeszkowiak. She also saw the film that night and she's blind too."

"I'm not sure we can now. We've got a plane to catch." He said looking quizzically at me.

"What's her number? I'll call her," I offered. "No answer. She's not home."

"What a pity. She lives in this road only a few houses down from here."

I looked at my watch. "We'll wait a couple of minutes and try again. If she's still not home we'll have to leave it. We wouldn't be able to finish in time to still get to the airport."

Fifteen minutes later we were in Pauline's lounge, camera rolling, and Mike was asking her to explain the extent of her blindness.

"They say it's less than 5%. Caused by macular degeneration. It's peripheral only, so if I turn to my side to look at you, I can see a blurred outline of where you are."

"Can you see me?" Mike asked.

"No, I know you are there but I can't see your face. It's like I can see an outline of a tree, very indistinctly, but I cannot see any leaves."

I zoomed in to her eyes in close up and they had a glazed milky look about them. They also had an unsettling steadiness, no quick shifting from far to near common with the functioning of healthy eyes.

"So why did you come to the hall that night, if you knew you wouldn't be able to watch the film?"

"I didn't know there would be a film. My friends told me that you were giving a talk and so I came along with them."

Like Harold, she then described the extraordinary thirty minutes during which her sight was restored completely. She too left us in no doubt that she had actually 'seen' the film.

"Can you explain why it happened?" Mike asked.

She didn't find it easy to express herself, making false starts, but finally she said in a very soft voice, "I think the grace of God came over me for some reason."

The priest who had been the master of ceremonies the night of the screening said in an interview, "If Harold clearly did see the film and he can give an account of what he saw, and if the medical evidence is that he should not have been able to see it, I think this is a further sign that this video is powerful, and is important as a proclamation of the truth and clearly had an impact in Adelaide that night. I would say that the video has made me even more conscious now than I was before of the great privilege I have as a priest to confect the Eucharist."

In a more considered tone he concluded that, "If a blind person was able to see the film, then you can take it as a sign from God that He wants the film seen."

He didn't know about the day in Miami we decided to make this film. He didn't know just how interesting his words were.

I cast my mind back to 12 May 2002, almost 18 months earlier, and Mike, Ricardo, Katya, Father Renzo and I were in Miami discussing a video that Ricardo had made on the Eucharist. While it had played Ricardo had translated the Spanish for Mike and myself. At the end of the tape we were all making comments and giving personal responses, all except for Katya who remained silent. When she finally spoke it was in a very sweet and sincere way: "Jesus," she said, "has asked that Mike you give to Ricardo your opinion."
"It's …um.." Mike hesitated, and weighing his response to the unseen Audience with a solicitous empathy for Ricardo said politely, "it's very good."
"No, Mike," Katya insisted, "Jesus has asked for Mike to give his professional opinion," and she underlined the word 'professional'.
Mike looked sheepishly at the floor. We all waited as he wrestled with how not to hurt his friend's feelings. When the words came they were direct and uncensored.
"The story you tell is excellent. But it is, I think, too long. You have written your script as if you were writing a book. Also there are too many images in quick succession; not enough pauses for people to digest what you are presenting." He collected his observations in a final statement. "Ricardo, it is difficult to make what you have done work with television."
Ricardo nodded, listening carefully. Mike felt exposed, and we all, (all except Katya), felt uncomfortable even if the 'professional' critique was certainly valid. When Katya spoke it was a relief, but at the same time placed us all in the unusual consciousness of being

Blind Harold O'Shea tells what he saw. (Coincidently Pauline Grzeszkowiak in shot)

Harold O'Shea

Pauline Grzeszkowiak

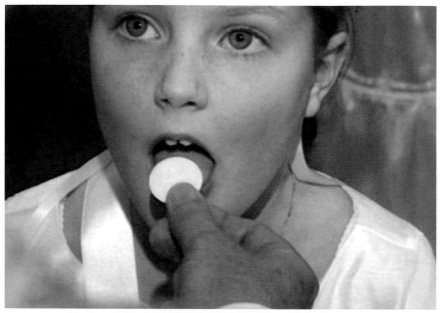

The "special" shot of the young girl receiving Holy Communion

present to and with a God that was closer than our thoughts and intimately involved with the world as it is.

"Jesus also says, *'Mike I agree with you.'* "

This made me smile. The casual conversational tone with which my God humbly shared in our discussion was delightful. It was as if he were sitting in a chair in the room, drinking coffee with us, looking and listening as we spoke, and contributing his observations. The biblical scene of the archangel Gabriel telling the Virgin Mary that her son was to be called 'Emmanuel', meaning 'God is with us', acquired a new and poignant immediacy. Jesus was with us, gently insisting on truth and the courage it demands.

"Now Mike," continued Katya as she related the instructions of our unseen Companion, *"make an English version and launch the film in Sydney in August this year. Also make the film so that it can reach the greater part of humanity."*

That 'greater part of humanity' it seems included even the blind. Who would have thought of making a film for the blind? And who would have thought that the 'greater part of humanity' included those Catholics one would imagine had least need of it: priests and religious? One such religious was Sister M. Baptista McCarthy. She saw it and said:

"What have I done to deserve such a treat? Actually, nothing! The good Lord knew how much I needed it! I have been in Religious Life for sixty two years….. You guessed it , I'm in my 83rd year! I have prepared children for the Sacraments during my teaching years. I have listened to sermons on the Eucharist, listened to theologians, scholars, noted preachers, retreat directors. All speak on this very profound doctrine…. Very sincerely too. But in no way did they impress me as did the talks you gentlemen gave. Thank you for bringing me to a realization and appreciation of what the Eucharist really means in my life!

To think I had to wait until my 83rd year of life to discover such a treasure…. But worth the long wait."

As filmmakers we merely followed orders. The appreciative reception the video enjoyed has been beyond our imagination Already it has been broadcast in many countries across the world. It has been translated into a number of languages. In Poland it elicited an unbelievable response from one of the Bishops who not only recommended that it be shown throughout the country but that it should be placed next to the Bible in every home! EWTN, a worldwide Catholic television network in America now shows it as a special program on the Feast of Corpus Christi each year. In my mind there is no doubt that the 'Executive Producer' of the work was as instrumental in its inception as in its reception and distribution, all of which have been truly beyond my imagination, comprehension or capacity.

CHAPTER 18

THE HEART
OF THE MATTER

Learn from me for I am meek and humble of heart.

Witnessing and also filming so many startling events had, over the years, naturally aroused in me amazement and awe. These however would have remained of little value had they not ignited a quest to understand their meaning. Katya's messages certainly provided many answers but they were not new or isolated islands of explanation. What I discovered as I pursued this work was how seamlessly and eloquently these apparent miracles reiterated and complemented the message given by Christ and by the Church as it developed in time. Even more, I learned how these contemporary events confirmed devotions the Church has promoted in the past.

Jesus promised that He would be with us until the end of time. Many interpret this as a vague sort of being-with-us in spirit, in moral support, in prayer, in uplifting togetherness of like-minded Christians. The Catholic Church however maintains that it is of supreme significance that God's only Son became a human being and that God's presence was therefore in the flesh, or more correctly stated, incarnational. God, a pure spirit, became matter for our sake, because we are feeble creatures who need sensible aids to our faith. That he was ridiculed, rejected and killed did not prevent a handful of believers from clinging to what they had seen. They saw him after his death. Alive! They became his heralds. For his sake they suffered trials, persecutions and martyrdom. No one would endure all this for a lifeless spectre. They believed in him as the source of their strength and went through the world in an act of incredible courage to share the good news he brought. Defying all the odds they succeeded in converting a significant portion of the known world.

What that good news declared was that he had chosen to offer himself as a perfect sacrifice, innocent and without complaint, on our behalf, knowing that his act of love would serve to pay the price for our being able to be with God in Heaven. But this act of love would not just happen once and for all time on a hill outside Jerusalem 2000 years ago. It was an eternal act, outside time, and would be remembered daily, on millions of altars around the world where the sacrificial victim would become again a living person, really present. The promise then that he would be with us is believed quite literally by Catholics.

The Old Testament tradition of God's people involved the daily sacrifice of livestock in the Temple. These burnt offerings were then consumed as their way of participation. The Church contends that the sacrifice of the Holy Mass is a daily 'unbloody' offering of the perfect victim to God for the atonement due to him for our sins, for the choices we make which exclude him. In effect God, in the consecrated host, is offered to God for our redemption.

We had evidence of living heart tissue in the Argentine host. What we had discovered scientifically was a material witness to a living heart. Three hundred years ago there was no such possibility for science to corroborate piety to the extent that today's technology allows. Nonetheless it was at that time in France that a devotion became popular in the Church which has continued to our day, the devotion to the Sacred Heart of Jesus.

A devotion is a special honour paid to some particular sacred person, or sacred thing, for a particular reason. The devotion to the Sacred Heart honours both Jesus' material heart of flesh and blood, the same heart that was born in a human baby and pierced by a Roman lance, and the heart as a symbol universally understood as the seat of love. Because the crowning act of his life was his voluntarily offering Himself for the redemption of all men, the symbol of the Sacred Heart restored the memory of his Passion as an act of great love.

Seventeenth century France was swamped by social unrest, dissension and a heresy which was driving Catholics from the Mass. This heresy, known as Jansenism, assaulted the traditional teaching of the Church. Firstly it denied that Christ died for all men. 'Not all men are created with a similar destiny; but eternal life is foreordained for some and eternal damnation for others,' said John Calvin, who shared this fallacy with the founder of the heresy, Cornelius Jansenius. Secondly it replaced a God of love with one of anger and vengeance. Extraordinary penance on behalf of the faithful was demanded. No one, it declared, 'not yet entirely perfect and perfectly irreproachable' should be allowed to partake of communion. This extreme rigour was disastrous for Mass attendance. People stopped going and stopped receiving Christ. Horrified, St Vincent de Paul wrote, 'We no longer see persons frequenting the Sacraments, not even at Easter, the way they formerly did.'

At the summit of this sweeping heresy, on 27 December 1673, an unassuming Visitation nun, then known as Margaret-Mary Alacoque, experienced the first of three great apparitions of Christ Himself. Each revelation commenced while she was in the presence of the Blessed Sacrament, the consecrated host. In the visions Jesus showed her His Heart and the messages revolved around the theme of His Heart suffering because of man's ingratitude and indifference.

Basilica Of Sacre Coeur, Paris

*Jesus appears to St Margaret Mary
and shows her His heart
(Painting, Vatican Museum)*

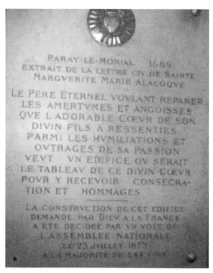

*Plaque inside the Basilica recording
vote of National Assembly*

He said,

"Behold this Heart which has loved men so much that it has spared nothing, even to exhausting and consuming itself in order to testify to them its love. In return I receive from the greater number nothing but ingratitude by reason of their irreverence and sacrileges and by the coldness and contempt which they show me in this Sacrament of Love."

In another appearance He asked her to convey a special request to the French monarch, King Louis XIV, that he co-operate in promoting the devotion. The image of His Sacred Heart was to be displayed in his palace, painted on his standards and engraved on his coat-of-arms. Christ had been vilified and condemned in the courts and palaces of his time. Now he wanted the honour that was his due in just such lofty places. Margaret-Mary wrote,

'He wants to be honoured there as much as He was outraged, condemned, and humiliated in His Passion, and to receive as much pleasure at seeing the great ones of the earth abased and humble before Him as He felt the bitterness by seeing Himself spurned at their feet.'

The next two hundred years of bloody revolution, terror, wars and civil unrest in France reflect the King's response to the message. He ignored it. But eventually the powers-that-be could do so no longer.

Millions of tourists to Paris visit a landmark structure in Montmartre, the beautiful white basilica of Sacre Coeur, (Sacred Heart) where the Eucharist is worshipped in perpetual adoration for twenty four hours every day of the year. Prominently displayed on the right hand wall is a stone plaque which records a resolution made by the French Parliament in 1873.

It reads: 'In light of the disasters that have fallen upon France we humble ourselves before God and we unite in our love of the Church admitting that we have been culpable and have been justly chastised. And to make amends for our sins and to obtain the infinite mercy of the Sacred Heart of Jesus we promise to contribute to Paris a sanctuary of the Sacred Heart.'

Adjoining it a plaque reads, 'The construction of this building demanded of France by God was decided by a vote of the National Assembly on 23 July 1873 by a majority of 244 votes.'

I was quite surprised when I read it. Life and politics are so thoroughly secularised today that it seemed inconceivable that little more than a hundred years ago a government reviewed its disastrous past not as a result of failures on the part of previous governments but as the inevitable outcome for its spiritual disobedience. Their conclusion, in the modern idiom, was astonishing. But even more so was their commitment to erect a magnificent basilica as a plea for mercy.

I was brought to remember the solutions for world peace given by the Virgin Mary at Fatima. God had a way out of current world crises and yet we have largely ignored it. The miracle of the Argentine host now seemed to be yet another intervention of God to call us to His way. It was a calculated intervention designed for a world transfixed in a purely materialist, science-based ideology. We only believe what we can see and touch and what science tells us is true. Therefore the miracle incorporates this need by its incarnational aspect. In the Argentine case it was science which told us the Eucharist is real flesh. It is a real heart.

Remember that as a result of the Eucharistic miracle of the 1200's, the miracle at Orvieto, the then Pope instituted a special feast day of

Corpus Christi. Mention of this day cropped up in the Sacred Heart story as well, for it was on this Feast in 1675 that Jesus requested of St Margaret-Mary that the Friday within the octave of the feast of Corpus Christi should be set aside in honour of his Sacred Heart. He wanted men to make amends to him on that day for those who offend him and cause his heart to suffer. The suffering is caused, he said, by the irreverence and disrespect which arose out of a general lack of belief in the Real Presence in the Eucharist.

On reading this something struck a chord in my memory. I remembered the words Jesus had said to Katya when Mike and I and a whole camera crew arrived in Bolivia to film the much anticipated stigmata.

"Tell Mike and Ron this is not the right time. Learn to trust in Me more. Tell them to come back on the day after the Feast of Corpus Christi and Mike will be able to film what he needs."

Besides being disappointed we were puzzled by the circuitous description of the day we were to return. At the time I had to find out when the Feast of Corpus Christi was and then add a day. It worked out to be two months away on 4 June. Why, I wondered, did Jesus simply not say to come back on 4 June? The 4 June, the day we returned, the day Katya was filmed during the entire experience of receiving the stigmata was Friday the feast of the Sacred Heart.

I was convinced that the purpose in this was to draw attention to the revelations he gave to St Margaret-Mary and that whatever was to happen on 4 June, the feast of the Sacred Heart more than three hundred years later, should be understood in relation to his request for that special commemoration. God, once again, chose to express his purpose materially in space, and now, I learned, also in time.

I went back to the contemporary messages given to Katya, and found that they were echoes from the past, from the messages given to St Margaret-Mary Alacoque.

'I offered myself to fulfill the work of redeeming the world. Ah, what a moment it was when I felt those torments come over Me, the torments I was to suffer in my Passion, the slander, the insults, the scourging, the kicks, the Crown of Thorns, the Cross.... All that passed before my eyes at the same time that an intense pain hurt My Heart: the offences, the sins, and the abominations that would be committed in the passing of time.... This Heart of Mine suffers because each day the number of sins that are committed is greater; greater each time are the sufferings that afflict it filling it with bitterness. You do not know, nor could you imagine the number of sins, blasphemies and sacrileges, the lukewarmness and indifference of so many souls that call themselves kind and their compassion is only a cover for hypocrisy.

My Heart is a burning furnace, passionate with Love for the salvation of souls. It bleeds and suffers. Day after day men go on accumulating iniquities for their own damnation. This is my torment.' [1]

(1) The Crusade of Love (81)

CHAPTER 19

LOVE'S SECOND NAME

The Sacred Heart devotion was a Divine remedy for the spiritual ailments of the seventeenth century, and had endured to our own. In the twentieth century, our own times, I was to learn of a relatively new devotion which arose from a corner of Europe which hadn't enjoyed much world attention until the millennium neared it's end: Poland.

From Poland came an electrician who rallied his disgruntled fellow workers of the Gdansk shipyard to demonstrate against communism under banners depicting the Virgin Mary. From Poland came the first non-Italian Pope for hundreds of years. He consecrated his priesthood to the Virgin Mary. Between the two of them, or should I say three of them, a pivotal event played out in Poland which quietly caused Eastern European Communism to crumble into the pile of rubble that was the Berlin Wall. It all happened not with a bang but with a pathetic whimper and the background roar of silent prayers. From Poland too came a nun whose mystical experiences would germinate into a devotion which proclaims the particular spiritual medicine for our current age: Divine Mercy.

The Latin word for 'mercy' is 'misericordia' which translates literally as 'suffering of the heart'. From this we get an understanding of mercy being the pain of one person for the pain of the other. But it goes further than compassion or empathy. Mercy means taking pain to do something about the pain of the other.

In a series of visions between 1931 and 1938, Jesus revealed to this nun that his mercy is unlimited and available to even the greatest sinner. The nun's name was Sister Faustina, the same woman whose diaries inspired my daughter's prayer at her grandmother's deathbed. All the messages are pertinent. If God is insistently offering us his mercy then what does that say about us, about what he sees in his creatures of the third millennium? From Faustina's hand we read:

'Write, the greater the sinner the greater the mercy. Summon all those to confidence in the incomprehensible depth of my mercy for I desire to save all. The well of Mercy was opened wide with a lance on the Cross, for all souls. I do not exclude anyone.......All misery vanishes in My Mercy, and every grace, redemptive and sanctifying, stems from this source. In the Old Covenant I sent prophets wielding thunderbolts to my people. Today I am sending you with My Mercy to the people of the whole world. I do not want to punish mankind, but I desire to heal it, pressing it to my Merciful Heart.' (1)

'... Step into the chapel for a moment and adore the Blessed Sacrament, My Heart which is full of Mercy.' (2)

'My daughter, know that My Heart is Mercy itself.' (3)

It took years after the death of Sister Faustina before the messages she received were acknowledged by the Church. But within it some men and women championed her authenticity from the outset. One of them was a young Polish priest recently elected a bishop. His name was Karol Wojtyla, the very same man who as Pope John Paul II would preside over her canonization on 30 April 2000. At this solemn ceremony he declared, "Today my joy is truly great in presenting the life and witness of Sister Faustina Kowalska to the whole church as a gift of God for our time....Indeed the message she brought is the appropriate and incisive answer that God wanted to offer to the questions and expectations of human beings in our time." He then continued to quote Jesus' message verbatim:

"Humanity will not find peace until it turns trustfully to Divine Mercy......Through the mystery of this wounded Heart, the restorative tide of God's merciful love continues to spread over the men and women of our time. Here alone those who long for true and lasting happiness find its secret."

One of the principal sources of the Church's teaching on mercy is the biblical scene of Jesus' death, where he hangs on a cross between two convicted criminals. One of them, Dismas, realised that Jesus was more than just innocent. Hearing Jesus forgive his executioners while in extreme suffering was an epiphany which led to the most famous last minute conversion of all. Jesus' exact words struck a chord which resonates even today. *Father forgive them for they know not what they do.* Dismas then begged Jesus to, *remember me when you go into your Kingdom.* Jesus responded, *This day you will be with me in Paradise.*

In dictation received by Katya Rivas, Jesus elaborates on the same encounter:

My Heart, tormented by suffering, had a feeling of compassion for another being who was suffering next to Me. The crucified man at my right, Dismas, called 'the good thief', kept watching Me with compassion; he who was also suffering. With one look, I increased the love in that heart. A sinner, yes, but capable of feeling compassion for another man. That wrongdoer, that bandit who hung from a cross, was another Magdalene, another Matthew, another Zaccheus, another sinner who was acknowledging Me as the Son of God. And that is why I wanted him to accompany Me toward Paradise that same afternoon, to be with Me, when I opened the doors of Heaven to give entrance to the Just. That was My mission and that is your mission: to open the doors of Heaven to sinners, to the repentant ones, to the men and women who are able to ask for forgiveness, to lay their hope in the existence of eternal life and place it next to My Cross. Dismas, the 'good' thief at My right, and Gestas the 'bad' thief at the left; the one on the left full of hatred; the one on My right changed in an instant upon hearing Me say these words: Father, forgive them for they know not what they do. That man, before My serene Presence, My suffering Presence, the Presence of the bearer of Peace, felt many things break inside of him. There was no longer any place for hatred. There was no place for sin, for violence, for bitterness.

Only a good heart is capable of acknowledging that which comes from heaven. Dismas was acknowledging it to himself. I was asking for forgiveness for those who were crucifying Me. I was pleading for Mercy for a sinner like him. And his little soul opened up to accept that Mercy. (4)

Pope John Paul II heeded the request made by Jesus through St Faustina by instituting a new feast for the calendar. The first Sunday after Easter was henceforth to be known as Divine Mercy Sunday, a day given to liturgical celebration of God's mercy. On Divine Mercy Sunday the world's billion Catholics recall the Gospel scene of the resurrected Jesus appearing to his fearful disciples in a locked room. Pope John Paul II spoke of the scene during the canonization of Saint Faustina. 'Jesus shows his hands and his side. He points, that is, to the wounds of the Passion, especially the wound in his heart, the source from which flows the great wave of mercy poured out on humanity. From that heart, Sister Faustina Kowalska, the Blessed who from now on we will call a saint, saw two rays of light shining and illuminating the world. The two rays, Jesus himself explained to her one day, represent blood and water.'

The Pontiff was taking us to the scene where Jesus appeared to Faustina bearing the wounds of his Passion, but wearing a white garment with his right hand raised in blessing and his left touching his garment covering his heart. Jesus desired that an image be painted as she saw him then. This image, now known as the Divine Mercy image, is in wide circulation and is venerated by those who seek the blessings and promises Jesus attached to it.

I found it interesting that God wanted an image made of himself. He sought not to be depicted as a glorious transcendent king but rather as a human person resurrected from the dead exhibiting his wounds: the stigmata and his pierced heart. On the other side of the world the same wounds were broadcast to millions of intrigued viewers as they appeared on the hands and feet of Katya Rivas. I recalled the words He spoke to Katya. *I have been preparing you for this day because I needed to reach the world one more time to show the world my suffering through a person like you. Thank you.*

On the first Divine Mercy Sunday Jesus showed his apostles his wounds that they might believe. And again, in our time, Jesus was generously, mercifully, showing the world his wounds that we might believe. The opportunity he offers is, I believe, undeniably underscored by the prime contemporary advocate of the message of Divine Mercy, Pope John Paul II himself.

In the voluminous and challenging written legacy of John Paul II one finds theology, philosophy and literature in which the theme of mercy is paramount. One encyclical, 'Dives in Misericordia', (Rich in Mercy) concentrates entirely on this aspect of God's nature. In it he wrote of the mercy denied to Jesus in His Passion, to a man, who being innocent, was so eminently deserving of mercy. He whose whole life and death was an act of Divine Mercy.

In the early hours of Divine Mercy Sunday in 2005 I was in my study busy at work on this very chapter. The news came that Pope John

*Original painting of the Divine Mercy image requested by Jesus of St Faustina
(Divine Mercy Shrine in Krakow)*

*Jesus shows His wounds to the Apostles
(Painting; Church of Santa Croce of Jerusalem, Rome)*

Paul II had died, he who had from the outset championed the message of a merciful God. The poetic coincidence and significance of the day of his death was not lost on me nor, as the foreign news reports came in, on the Church. I myself couldn't help but see the timing of this great pope's death on Divine Mercy Sunday as an intentional act of God drawing attention to the Pope's great energy in promoting the Divine Mercy message to the contemporary world. It was as if God was highlighting this as the Pope's last will and testament in the hope that we may read it and follow it as a solution for the conflicts which ravaged our world.

Catholics knew just how truly great a leader he had been. But so too it seems did the secular world. It was the largest gathering of mourners for any funeral ever before. Millions and millions of mourners flooded into Rome. International networks covering the event trained their cameras on the major world leaders who had all converged on Rome for the funeral. There they all were, from every continent: George Bush, Bill Clinton, Vladimir Putin, Tony Blair, Kofi Annan, Jacques Chirac, Gerhard Schroeder, King Juan Carlos, Mohammed Khatami, Bashar al-Assad, Moshe Katsav; leaders present and past, the movers and shakers in whose political hands rested the well-being or otherwise of most of the planet. I scrutinised them closely as they stood next to the simple wooden coffin and felt strongly that they had been touched, moved in some way or other by the life and work of John Paul II. From them, from the leaders of the secular world, came the acclaim that he was, in the words of Henry Kissinger, "the greatest human being of our time; he was the only universal leader we had and he gave a sense of direction to the world at large."

A strange and sad irony lingered in this scene of the power brokers beside the coffin. They were the ones we all trusted with finding solutions for world peace. And yet their ways to peace were often in contradiction to the figure who lay before them. Their way included 'pre-emption' and 'retaliation' and 'collateral damage' whilst his spoke of mercy, of forgiving your enemy. He had written,

'Jesus Christ taught that man not only receives and experiences the mercy of God, but that he is called to practise mercy towards others. Blessed are the merciful for they shall obtain mercy. Man attains to the merciful love of God, his mercy, to the extent that he himself is interiorly transformed in the spirit of that love toward his neighbour.' (5)

'Modern man' he continues, 'often anxiously wonders about the solution to the terrible tensions which have built up in the world and which entangle humanity. And if at times he lacks the courage to utter the word 'mercy', or if in his conscience, empty of religious content, he does not find the equivalent, so much greater is the need for the Church to utter this word, not only in her own name but also in the name of all the men and women of our time'

Appealing to a modern world which proclaims in various ways that God is superfluous he says, 'If any of our contemporaries do not share the faith and hope which lead me, as a servant of Christ and steward of the mysteries of God, to implore God's mercy for humanity in this hour of history, let them understand the reason for my concern. It is dictated by love for man which according to the intuition of many of our contemporaries is threatened by an immense danger…. It obliges me to have recourse to God's mercy and to beg for it at this difficult, critical phase of the history of the Church and of the world…' (6)

How many of those so-called 'peacemakers' present at that Vatican funeral could believe that the world's conflicts and its attendant dangers could be averted by a spiritual solution? And that that spiritual solution was advocated by the man who now lay silent before them? With courage, absolute conviction, and practical determination he himself had followed it knowing that it came from Christ and was urgently repeated through the revelation given to Saint Faustina: Mercy.

The means to obtain peace without conflict is the goal of the true peacemaker. This profound teaching Jesus gave is beautifully expressed in his message to Katya. In this selection from 'The Door to Heaven' he says:

A long time ago, housewives would carefully gather pieces of burning coal, placing them in the middle of the fire so the flame would not die out. In the same way, you should gather all the energies of peace and love and place them in yourselves and in your relationships with your neighbours, particularly when they give you difficulties.

A non-violent act in favour of peace does not seek to annihilate the adversary, but to make him a common friend of peace. If there is an inner energy inside you and you believe in My action that cultivates thoughts of peace, you must not distrust your adversary. You should make him understand that inside him there also exists a profound desire for peace and justice. In this way, you will be helping him to discover the good that exists inside him.

You have been talking for so many years of a moral re-armament that would have precedence over any material rearmament.... You have so much more. You have the God of peace and the Gospel of peace.

Begin now. Learn to discover the internal sources of peace and to build on them the art of the non-violent solution to disputes. Learn the art of telling the truth with love, even when injustice, violence and hypocrisy must be unmasked." [7]

(1) The Diary of Sister Faustina (1588)
(2) Ibid (1572)
(3) Ibid (1777)
(4) From Sinai to Calvary
(5) Papal Encyclical: Dives in Misericordia (139)
(6) Ibid
(7) Door to Heaven

CHAPTER 20

SCIENCE
AND AN OLD
EVANGELISATION

One man who read and accepted the messages Katya was receiving was Monsignor Rene Fernandez, the Bishop of Cochabamba. On 8 August 1996 Jesus asked for a Marian Eucharistic Congress to be held. The Bishop organized just such a congress. Various delegates from both North and South America were present and all received documents distributed by the Bishop. These were inspired in their spiritual content by Katya's messages. The fruit of this congress was the formation, in 1999, of a new international apostolate which would be called the Apostolate for the New Evangelization, or the ANE. At its head Bishop Fernandez appointed Father Renzo Sessolo, the very same priest assigned to Katya as her spiritual director, the same priest from whom came the miraculous host which was given to my mother on her deathbed.

The call was precipitated by the visit of the most highly respected authority of the Catholic Church who visited Mexico in January 1999. Pope John Paul II recognised the need for a new evangelisation, 'not new in content, but in its methods, in its forms and ardour to bring men to the feet of our Lord.' Now again he vigorously re-stated his wish and spoke of the 21st century as being 'the century of the new evangelisation.' In an impassioned plea he spoke to the people of the Americas, and to Catholics around the world, to come forward for recruitment to this pressing need.

'As followers of Christ, we long for unity not division, for brotherhood and not antagonism, for peace and not war to prevail in the coming century. This is also an essential goal of the new evangelisation. As the Church's children you must work so that the coming global society is not spiritually impoverished or heir to the mistakes of the century now ending. The new evangelisation will be a seed of hope for the new millennium if you, todays Catholics, make the effort to transmit to future generations the precious legacy of human and Christian values which have given meaning to your lives. Show that Christ has the words of eternal life. Reveal to your brothers and sisters the divine and human face of Jesus Christ, the alpha and the omega, the beginning and the end, the first and the last of all creation and all history, even of the history you are writing with you own lives.'

The patron of this Apostolate of the New Evangelization would be, as proclaimed by Pope John Paul II that same day in Mexico City, the Virgin Mary, Our Lady of Guadalupe and Queen of the New Evangelization. The 12 December, the feast day of Our Lady of Guadalupe would be the anniversary of the ANE. It was the exact day my mother was given the miraculous host, by the man who was appointed the head of the ANE, a gift of Jesus himself, a gift of three more years of life.

The Holy Father reminded his audience of an unprecedented and astonishing evangelization which was spear-headed from Mexico four and a half centuries before. In only eight years nine million people converted to the Catholic Church! That's an average of three thousand baptisms a day. It stands as one of history's most radical, monumental and rapid social transformations ever.

It all began on the 9 December 1531, and in God's preferred way of working, it began with a humble, illiterate, completely powerless and very poor human being. Juan Diego was an Aztec Indian, an aboriginal, in a country recently conquered by Spain. The conquest of central and South America had involved some unspeakable acts of cruelty and rabid greed on the part of the imperialist armed forces, administrators and bounty hunters. It was little wonder that the mostly sincere and well-meaning missionaries that accompanied the Spanish expeditions made little headway in converting the resistant native Indian population to the faith of their oppressors. Juan Diego was one of the few who was converted and he was on his way to catechism on that fateful day when his life and the future of the entire South American continent changed forever.

He was trudging through a barren, stony and desolate landscape near what is now Mexico City, when he heard, coming from the top of a little hill known as Tepeyac, strange and beautiful music. Then he heard his name being called. Of course he went up to investigate and there encountered a luminous beautiful lady whose garments glittered with colours and which radiated reflected light on the ground and rocks around her. It was unearthly yet he felt no fear. She spoke to him in his native tongue in words which were charming and affectionate.

"Juanito, the smallest of my children, where are you going?" she asked.

He responded reverently and she introduced herself.

"Know this as true. I am the perfect ever-virgin Mary mother of the most true God through whom everything lives, the creator of persons, the master of closeness and proximity, the master of heaven and earth. I am the Mother of Him whom we love."

She instructed him to tell the local Bishop, Bishop Zumarraga, of her apparition and to request the building of a church on that very site from which her children would receive special graces and blessings.

"Lady, smallest of my daughters, my child," he responded in a beautifully humble local idiom, "please choose someone else, someone important. My Lady, you send me where I have no place, no standing."

But she consoled him with a promise of assistance.

Upon hearing the ragged peasant's story the Bishop was not exactly dismissive, but prudently suspicious. He asked Juan Diego for some proof of his unusual encounter. There followed a fascinating series of events: the Bishop's spies were foiled in attempting to follow Juan Diego; then Juan Diego avoided the agreed appointment with 'the lady' because he was urgently seeking a priest to assist at his uncle's deathbed; then he avoided the meeting place because he hoped she would choose someone of greater stature than himself; and finally she herself found him out. The sign would be given, she promised, by him going to the top of the hill and gathering up the flowers that bloomed there. He complied although he already knew the place to be arid and that no flowers, nor any other plants for that matter, had ever grown there. Furthermore, it was the middle of winter. In the designated rocky place, to his amazement, he found in gorgeous abundance, a veritable garden of lush Castillian roses. He plucked as many as he could hold and when his arms were too full he removed his tilma, a coarsely woven cape commonly worn by the Indians, and placed them in it.

The Bishop's attendants refused him access and insisted on seeing the contents of his bundle. The roses tumbled out. The attendants went to examine them but each time their hands went to grasp a rose it would mysteriously vanish into thin air. Three times they tried. Three times they failed. Bewildered, and frightened they quickly ushered Juan Diego into the Bishop's office. There, in the presence of Bishop Zumarraga and his interpreter Juan Gonzales, Juan Diego again repeated the Lady's request for a church. This time he opened his tilma and the roses cascaded to the floor. The Bishop was absolutely amazed. He and the interpreter fell prostrate before Juan Diego who was holding his empty tilma out in front of him. Juan Diego wondered why so little attention was being paid to the heavenly flowers and their lingering fragrance, and why they were staring at his old garment. He turned it around and then he too fell to his knees in awe. What he and the others beheld on the 12th December 1531 would baffle and inspire worshippers, scientists, and even revolutionaries for the next five hundred years.

On his tilma, measuring 4ft by 7ft, a miraculous image had appeared of itself. In it a beautiful young indigenous woman, clothed in a garment of stars and standing on a burnt-out crescent moon, was praying. The Bishop was entirely convinced of Juan Diego's story and proceeded to consecrate the site of the apparition and build the church the Heavenly Mother had requested.

There, the same image continues to be the magnet for over 7 million pilgrims a year. No other Catholic site, outside of Rome, has so many visitors. Miracles, blessings and graces are said to flow from it to the faithful. The most startling of these was when a dead man was raised to life as he was brought before the image on 25 December 1531. This singular miraculous event was verified by the large assembled crowd and news of it quickly spread popular devotion. Many thousands of conversions ensued.

The Aztecs at that time 'wrote' in pictures. Recorded communication was pictographic and not, as in the west, alphabetical. In the miraculous image they read an intelligible and powerfully persuasive message to abandon their traditional religion for the new faith. From it they effortlessly interpreted a supernatural revelation depicted in familiar symbols correlating to their own existing religious worldview. The arrangement of stars on her mantle, for instance, was instantly significant to a culture in which sophisticated astronomical

Pope John Paul II before Our Lady of Guadalupe Mexico (Courtesy ClaraVision Mexico)

observation played a major role. The image proved to be a rare text bridging disparate continents and religions. It was, to an ancient Aztec civilisation, entirely convincing. It was enough to compel conversion of nine million people in under a decade.

The Aztecs believed that gods created the world and that the 'birth' of the sun was the most important act of creation. The only way to ensure its continuation was by appeasing their deities through human sacrifice. The gods were to be fed with the divine substance: human blood. Many ethnographers, scholars and historians have estimated that over 100 000 sacrifices were made annually, with the figure of 250 000 victims considered a conservative estimate. This heavy spiritual burden came to end with the advent of Our Lady of Guadalupe and the mass conversion which followed.

In Aztec the word, 'coatlaxopeuh' means 'the one who crushes, breaks, stamps on, the serpent god.' When the Spanish speaking Bishop heard it spoken of as 'the Lady's' desired name he mistook it for the similarly pronounced, more familiar name of an ancient shrine dedicated to the Blessed Mother in 'Guadalupe', Spain. The image is now commonly known as 'Our Lady of Guadalupe'.

Through hundreds of years the image remains mysterious and continues to provoke attention, attention which is not only religious in nature. Scientists and even political revolutionaries have faced the mystery which deepens even as more and more is discovered.

By the early nineteen twenties Mexico was in the grip of a socialist revolution which denounced the reality of God and committed itself to a violent assault on all things religious, specifically the dominant Catholic Church. Churches were destroyed and barricaded, church properties were confiscated, and in an active reign of terror thousands of priests were left dead or exiled. One of the agents of the communist forces, Luciano Perez, gave a detailed first-hand account of the attack on the church in which the miraculous tilma was venerated. On the 14 November 1921 he had personally placed a very large bomb concealed in a gigantic vase of flowers directly below the suspended image. He was chosen for the job because of his powerful physique and the strength required to carry the weight of the vase packed with dynamite. The blast was enormous and its impact left the marble altar in smithereens, all the windows shattered, the windows across the road demolished too, paintings and statues reduced to rubble, and a large iron crucifix gnarled and buckled almost in half. It is still displayed today and is an impressive testament to the magnitude of the blast. But the intended target of the communist forces, the image of Our Lady of Guadalupe, under which the bomb was directly placed, remained unscathed. Not the slightest crack even marred its glass case. And as history subsequently showed, that moment was the turning point, the beginning of the end of the socialist revolution in Mexico.

Scientists too are confounded. How does a crude piece of fabric, woven from cactus fibre which in ordinary circumstances has a durability of no more than 20 years, last for over 400? For the first 116 years the tilma was exposed without any protection whatsoever. Yet it has remained resilient despite exposure to the gritty, salty winds and humidity of the Mexican climate, despite the chemical impact of the fumes of millions of votive candles, and despite the thousands of sweaty adoring hands which grasped at it so fervently as to pull out individual fibrous threads. Yet there is no loss to the integrity of the fabric or the image. An inexpert cleaning job on the silver frame in1791 even resulted in nitric acid being spilt on it yet the only remaining evidence of this highly corrosive chemical is a slight yellowish watermark which, according to experts, is inexplicably fading through time.

When, in 1963, photographs by Howard Earp, an American, revealed a few pinholes in the mantle of the image, it was possible for the first time to see a cross-section of the fabric. Most paintings have the pigment mixed with it's carrying medium being absorbed by the foundational material. For instance, the medium may be oil, tempera or water, and the foundation may be canvas or paper. The colour in its carrying medium then impregnates or is absorbed by the surface to which it is applied. Yet in this case, to the amazement of the examiners, the image lay on the maguey cloth without so much as slightly staining it. This is beyond the power of scientific explanation for the image and the fabric remain all of a piece, neither dissolving nor collapsing. One observer exclaimed, "It's as if it has been painted on thin air!" It is claimed that later laser examination revealed that there was no colouration on either the front or the back of the cloth and that the colours hover at a distance of 0.3mm from the cloth without touching it.

Richard Kuhn, the 1938 Nobel prizewinner for Chemistry examined two coloured fibres from the image, one reddish and the other yellow. He certified that 'in these two fibres there are neither vegetable, nor animal, nor mineral, much less synthetic colourings.'[1] In plain language the colourings do not exist on earth.

NASA researchers Smith and Callahan, using infrared photography began a study on Our Lady of Guadalupe on 7 May 1979. They report the blue of the mantle to be, 'made of an unknown semi-transparent pigment, unexplainable in density and in the absence of fading.'[2]

The colours have remained uncannily fresh. An ethereal effervescence, like shot silk, causes the image to almost shift and glow seeming remarkably lifelike. The same NASA report says 'the pink pigment appears to be inexplicable. One of the really strange aspects of the painting is that not only is the tilma unsized but it also has absolutely no protective coat or varnish Despite this the robe and the mantle are as brightly coloured as though they were newly painted.'[3]

Callahan concluded, 'For those of my readers who do not believe in the possibility of miracles I find no better solution than to end my study with the words that the great Catholic philosopher and writer G.K. Chesterton wrote in his short masterpiece *'Orthodoxy'*:

'My belief in miracles cannot be considered a mystical belief: it is founded on human evidence, as is my belief in the discovery of America. It is, indeed, a simple logical fact that hardly needs to be recognized or interpreted. The extraordinary idea going around is that those who deny the miracle know how to consider the facts coolly and directly, while those who accept the miracle always relate the facts with the dogma previously accepted. In fact, the opposite is the case: the believers accept the miracle (with or without reason) because the evidence compels them to do so. The unbelievers deny it (with or without reason) because the doctrine they profess compels them to do so.' ' (4)

Many of those who have examined it say that despite the global availability of photographic reproductions, nothing compares to the original which enjoys a sense of living presence, especially in the tenderness of the eyes. The common response to the living quality of the eyes may have been little more than the enthusiastic sentimentality of believers had not the advent of photography, revealed a secret hidden for over four hundred years.

Photographic enlargements made in 1929 uncovered the reflection of a person in the eyes. Later, in1965, Dr Rafael Lavoignet, examined the eyes with an ophthalmoscope to conclude that the eyes had the usual depth of real living eyes. When magnified twenty five times a group of human figures was revealed. It was, in his view, impossible to obtain such a reflection from a flat, and what is more, a dark surface. His findings were endorsed by a respected authority in optical sciences at the University of Colombia, Dr Frank Avignone.

Paintings by three different artists commissioned to memorialise Bishop Zumarraga blessing the newly built church on Tepeyac hill all depicted the Bishop, Juan Diego and Juan Gonzalez within their large group scenes. From these sixteenth century originals a large copy was painted and subsequently lost, only to resurface in the nineteen sixties. The characters painted clearly identify the figures reflected in the eyes: Juan Diego, the Bishop and his interpreter, those present at the moment the image appeared on the tilma. Work by engineer Aste Tonsman, a satellite imaging expert, using a computer enhanced photographic process known as image digitalization, discovered an enhanced and much magnified reflection in the cornea of the Virgin's eyes. It too was of the 1531 scene at the moment of the miraculous appearance of the image, only much more detailed.

In October 1996 my own curiosity drew me to Mexico City to film an interview with Dr Jorge Escalante, an ophthalmologist and surgeon who had practised as a specialist for 42 years. He spoke with insistence and conviction of his latest findings:

"The eyes have all the characteristics of a human eye. It has all the parts. Around the pupil are contraction furrows which operate to contract the pupil in front of light. These furrows were only detected by ophthalmologic science in the twentieth century. You can see the vascular supply in the upper eyelid of the right eye. When we discovered these blood vessels five years ago we were completely surprised. It is a snapshot of an eye, alive, with all its interior parts, like another human person. We are dealing with a human eye. It is not a picture. It is not a painting. It is impossible to have been created by man artificially."

The next subject I interviewed was Jaime Mausson, the well-known Mexican TV presenter who had produced a film on the image of our Lady of Guadalupe for '60 Minutes'. From behind his desk he said: "I did not believe in this miracle. But when we did the program for '60 Minutes' we realised there were many things that could not be explained about the image, especially the eyes. We put a big lens close to the virgin. I was alone looking at the eye. I saw the eyelashes, then I saw the blood vessels, all the veins. Then I looked into the iris and to the pupil and I had the sensation that I was seeing a live eye. I felt inside of me a voice that asked me, 'What do you want from me?' It was very shocking. I was seeing a live eye. I don't normally speak of my private emotions but I have to say that I realised at that moment that whatever was there was alive when that image was created and was alive then and was looking at me. That is the sensation I had. Whatever is there is still alive."

And this brings me back to the words spoken on Tepeyac to the 57 year old Indian all those years ago. Like the eyes they are very much still alive.

'I am your merciful mother, the merciful mother of all who live united in this land, and of all mankind, of all those who have confidence in me. Here I will pity their weeping, their sorrow, and will remedy and alleviate all their sufferings, necessities and misfortunes.'

The entirely unforeseen and remarkably swift evangelization of Mexico and the South American continent was catalyzed by a miraculous image of the Mother of God. Across the ocean on another continent is another, far older image, as miraculously created, and I believe, as potentially compelling for a whole new evangelization of humanity today.

(1)   Francis Anson   *Guadalupe- what her eyes say*
        English translation published by Sinag-tala Publishers, Inc., Manila in 1994
(2)   ibid
(3)   ibid
(4)   ibid

CHAPTER 21

SCIENCE AND A NEW EVANGELISATION

On 14 April 1995, the day Dr Ricardo Castanõn took the first blood sample from the statue of Christ in Bolivia for testing, Katya received the following message from Jesus:

"I want the blood that is wiped from My Image to be given to the Church authorities and for it to be compared with the blood of My Shroud. It is time for the lies to be buried and for the truth to be revealed."

I asked Katya, in a filmed interview, what she understood by that message. She replied, "I understand that when the blood from the statue is compared with the blood on the Shroud of Turin they will find that the blood is from the same person and that this will assist in the authentification of the Shroud of Turin as the true burial cloth of Jesus Christ."

"Do you realise," I asked, "what the consequences for you will be if the blood does not match?"

She replied with a soft smile, "I trust in my Lord."

The Shroud of Turin is probably the most thoroughly examined piece of linen in history, and, like the image of Our Lady of Guadalupe, continues to benefit from advances in science and technology. It bears two full length life size images, front and back, of a 5'11" man who has been scourged and crucified, wounds correlating in uncanny exactitude with Gospel accounts of the suffering and death of Jesus.

Pope John Paul II described it as, "one of the most unsettling signs of the Redeemer's love....a precious linen that can help us better understand the mystery of the love of God's Son for us. The shroud is a challenge to our intelligence. It first of all requires of every person, particularly the researcher, that he humbly grasp the profound message it sends to his reason and his life. .... Since it is not a matter of faith, the Church entrusts to the scientists the task of continuing to investigate so that satisfactory answers may be found to the question of the sheet, which according to tradition wrapped the body of our Redeemer.....In the incomparable suffering that it documents, the love of the One who *so loved the world that he gave his only Son'* is made almost tangible and reveals all its astonishing dimensions. In its presence believers can only exclaim in all truth; 'Lord, you could not love me more!' and immediately realise that sin is responsible for that suffering: the sins of every human being."

In 1898, shortly after the invention of photography the shroud was photographed for the first time. When the negative was seen it revealed an altogether unprecedented and irreproducible dimension which had lain hidden for 1900 years, hidden until man had invented the technology necessary for the startling, and to this day unaccountable, revelation. A positive three-dimensional image emerged on the negative plate. As if by magic, a real man could be clearly seen. The shroud itself turned out to be a negative waiting until the invention of photography could make a positive 'print' of what it held secret.
Then in the 1960's Leo Vala, a professional London photographer, used slide projectors to beam negatives of the shroud onto malleable plasticine. The resulting three dimensionality provoked

him to say, "I have been involved in the invention of many complicated visual processes and I can tell you that no-one could have faked that image. No-one could do it today with all the technology we have. It's a perfect negative. It has a photographic quality that is extremely precise." [1]

In the late seventies, an American physicist, Dr John Jackson gained access to the Interpretation Systems VP-8 Image Analyzer, a sophisticated device developed by NASA for its space projects. It translated a monochromatic tonal scale in photographed images to layers of vertical relief. When a still photograph is analyzed by the V8 it is invariably collapsed and distorted. But when the shroud image was analyzed it revealed an unusually consistent three dimensional effect. The intricacies of the technology are difficult to describe but for the scientists involved their discovery was nothing short of mind-blowing. The electronics engineer and inventor of V-8, Peter Schumacher, described the moment he first saw the shroud viewed via his system.

"A 'true three dimensional' image appeared on the monitor…. The nose ramped in relief. The facial features were contoured properly. Body shapes of the arms, legs and chest and the basic human form….. I had never heard of the Shroud of Turin before that moment. I had no idea what I was looking at. However the results are unlike anything I have processed through the VP-8 Image Analyzer before or since. Only the Shroud of Turin has ever produced these results."

Peter Schumacher's comments on the ever growing and bewildering evidence in the realm of scientific imaging are worth repeating.
"No method, no style, and no artistic skills are known to exist that can produce images that will induce the same photographic and photogrammetric results as the Shroud image induces….. The shroud image exhibits some properties of photographic negatives, some

properties of body frame imaging and some properties of three dimensional grey-scale encoding. It is 'none of these' and represents portions of 'all of these' and more." [2]

In the 1980's a chemist at Michigan University, Dr Giles Carter discerned that the shroud displayed properties shared with long-wave X-rays. He detected the skeletal structure of the bones in the hands as well as what appeared to be two rows of teeth.

1988 was a big year for the skeptics. Carbon dating results claimed that the shroud was medieval and a fake. The results were carried triumphantly throughout the world's press. But the scientific fascination with it did not cease. Subsequent analysis has shown beyond question that the samples used in these carbon dating tests were from a mended border which differs in weave and chemical composition from the main section of the cloth. The 1988 results which delighted skeptics have been comprehensively discredited. The general press has all but ignored these revisions and so many people remain in ignorance, whether innocent, complacent or arrogant. Not so the many scientists actively involved in continuing investigation.

Some have examined the shroud's chemical composition, some the dust and pollen residues, some the technology of the weave. Others have focused on the physical nature of crucifixion and its effects as predicted and confirmed by the shroud. But what interests me and my colleagues is the blood. Our main interest, and the work we are undertaking at present, focuses on the stains which occur at the location of the wounds. Whilst filming at a conference in Nice in1997 the report by Dr Alan Adler, a Jewish research chemist from the Western Connecticut State University, caught my particular attention.

"There is," he said, "No dye, pigment or stain making up the image of the man whose body you see on the cloth. It is not a painting. It simply represents chemically a dehydrative oxidative process of the cellulose of the fibres constructing the weave of the cloth. This discoloration is only one fibre deep on the crowns of the threads comprising the weave, which I point out to you, is half the thickness of the average human hair. The blood images on this cloth were put there by this cloth coming in contact with a man who was wounded and died a traumatic death. When you analyse the blood wounds you observe that you are not looking at whole blood, you are looking at the exudates of clotted wounds and furthermore there are some very peculiar features in the chemistry of these wounds and their composition: they contain an abnormally large amount of bilirubin. There is a very simple explanation for that. You are looking at a man who died a severely traumatic death prior to the shedding of this blood. In other words he was in traumatic shock, the kind of thing you would get if you were beaten and then crucified. Under these conditions you get an enormous so-called icric index of the bilirubin to the haemoglobin into the blood which, when it forms the clot, will be in the exudates from the clot, and will make the kind of wounds we see, in particular, the red colour."

The blood on the shroud is almost certainly degraded, having existed for two thousand years at most, or seven hundred years if one still gives any credence to the 1988 carbon dating tests. Either way it is extremely old. Should the Church permit new tests which validate the cloth as a burial shroud of a crucified man from Palestine in 30 AD, this in itself would not persuade the skeptic who can rightly claim that hundreds of men were crucified by the Romans in that part of the world at that time. Dr Alan Adler put the big question in a nutshell when he said, "The hypothesis 'Is this Jesus Christ?' is not experimentally testable. We do not have a laboratory test for Jesus Christness." [3]

What we have since discovered though is another chapter in the story of the blood of Christ, one which may well provide Dr Adler's elusive 'test for Jesus Christness'. Hundreds of experts have analysed the shroud for over a hundred years but only recently has a second relic become a fascinating piece of evidence in the 'test for Jesus Christness'. It provides another case for possible comparison with the shroud in determining identity through future analysis of degraded DNA. The more sources to draw from the better our chances. This one led us to yet another small town with one of the Church's best kept secrets.

In the town of Oviedo in Spain (not to be confused with Orvieto in Italy) is the Sudarium Domini, the Sudarium of our Lord. It is a blood stained linen cloth, about the size of a towel, that has existed in virtual obscurity for about 1200 years. Its relevance lies in it being the purported cloth mentioned in the Gospel of St John as the second linen, *'the cloth that had been over his head'*. This one was found still rolled up in a corner of the tomb on Sunday morning when John, the only apostle who was an eyewitness to the crucifixion and burial of Jesus, entered to find it. It was in the same place where it had been left on Good Friday when the crucified body of Jesus had been laid in the tomb. The shroud which had covered the body on the stone mortuary shelf was lying *'flattened'* or *'deflated'* (from the original Greek 'keisthai') whereas the other linen was rolled up and unchanged from where it had been placed before the disciples left and sealed the tomb on Friday evening. There was no body.

Here is the extract in question from John 20: 3 – 9
> *So Peter set out with the other disciple to go to the tomb. They ran together, but the other disciple, running faster than Peter, reached the tomb first; he bent down and saw the linen cloths lying on the ground and also the cloth that had been over his head: this was not with the linen cloths but rolled up in a place*

by itself. Then the other disciple who had reached the tomb first also went in. He saw and he believed. Till this moment they had not understood the scripture, that he must rise from the dead.

John goes to surprising length detailing the contrasting condition and position of the burial cloths because what he saw at that moment did not suggest to him that Jesus' body had been stolen. Instead he writes emphatically that, *he saw and he believed. Till this moment they had not understood the scripture, that he must rise from the dead.* What John saw was of such significance and so persuasive that it caused him to believe that a dead man had been resurrected. Jesus had repeatedly told his disciples that this was to happen and yet even John, the apostle who was closest to him, until that very moment didn't believe.

What is also interesting and not often discussed is what follows directly on in the next verses:
But Mary was standing outside near the tomb, weeping. Then as she wept she stooped to look inside and saw two angels in white sitting where the body of Jesus had been, one at the head and one at the feet.

Mary saw the angels seated in positions defined by their relation to where the body had been, and where, I would argue, the shroud still lay flattened so that the head and feet positions were perceptible. Why would she use anatomical words like 'head' and 'feet' if there was no corpse? She might just as well have said two angels were sitting on each end of the shroud, or on the mortuary shelf, or even simply in the tomb. The two cloths, from the very first have been coupled to convey an event which science today is still deconstructing to our edification and amazement.

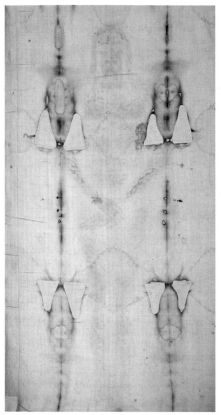

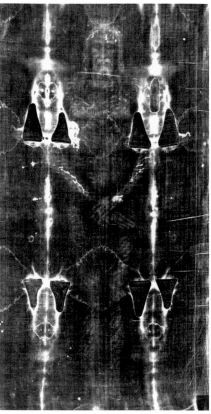

Front view of the Shroud
(© 1978 Barrie Schwortz)

Negative of the Shroud
(© 1978 Barrie Schwortz)

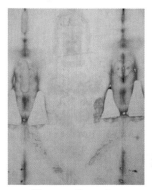

Close up front view
of the Shroud

Dr Alan Adler at Conference on the Shroud
(Nice France, 1997)

The Camera Santa, or Holy Chamber, in the Cathedral of Oviedo, built in the 8th Century to protect the Sudarium

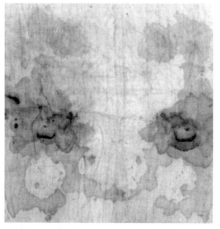

Blood stains on the Sudarium (Courtesy Goya Producciones, Madrid)

Mark Guscin demonstrates how the Sudarium was used on Jesus crucified

Veneration of the Holy Blood, Bruge Belgium

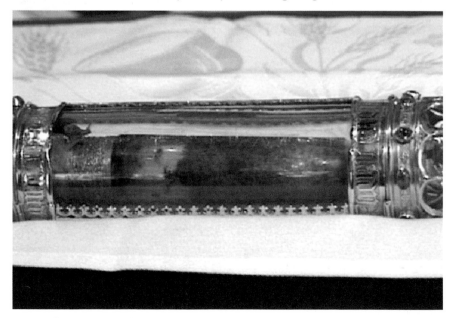

Vial containing Holy Blood, believed to be from the crucifixion: Bruge Belgium

The provenance of the Sudarium, the second cloth, and the history of its journey to Spain has been surprisingly straightforward. I met and filmed the historian Mark Guscin, one of the members of the team involved in these studies, and he produced copies of various manuscripts which give consistent accounts of its existence and its passage to Oviedo. They describe it as having been taken in a wooden trunk with other relics by presbyter Philip from Jerusalem for safekeeping from the invading Persians in 614. It travelled through North Africa to Cartegna in Spain. Microscopic pollen analysis by Dr Max Frei positively place it in areas which confirm this passage. In 710 it was again hidden from Muslim invaders in an inaccessible mountain cave in the village of Montsacro. Later a small chapel was built at the site and the trunk with it contents was concealed in a well under the altar. In 1075, after the Moors had been expelled, it was removed and a detailed inventory made in the presence of King Alfonso VI and a notable entourage. In 1113 the chest was overlaid with silver and inscribed with an invitation to the faithful to venerate the Holy Blood therein. It found a home in the specially built vault, the Camera Santa of the Cathedral of San Salvador, where it has remained ever since.

For much of its history keeping it safe meant keeping it secret. The Sudarium was only publicly exposed on a few rare occasions. Even kings were denied seeing it. You can imagine my delight then when huge medieval keys unlocked the wrought iron grille and we entered the ancient stone dungeon to film the silver chest. Multiply my delight a million times to euphoria when the sudarium was removed and laid out for us to see. I couldn't contain myself and very very slowly I deliberately touched the corner of the cloth. It felt coarse but incredibly thin and fine, almost papery. In my mind, at that moment, I saw the Michelangelo painting of Creation where the finger of Adam reaches up seeking to touch the finger of God. In my case I felt that our fingers touched.

Unlike the much more dramatic Shroud of Turin, which bore an image of Christ, the Sudarium shows, at first glance, only bloodstains of varying colour densities. This goes part of the way to explaining its occupying a backseat to the more spectacular shroud. But this is all changing and has been since 1989 when a team of scientists and experts in various scientific and academic fields agreed to collaborate. They work under the auspices of the Centro Espagnol de Sindonologia. They committed themselves to a comprehensive evaluation of the Sudarium, working only within their own areas of specialisation. After five years, in 1994, they presented their initial findings. Even so, the team declares its work is still in its infancy.

How and why the Sudarium was used has been established. Studies have shown that it was used in compliance with ancient Jewish funereal practices and in accordance with Jewish religious concepts concerning blood, the soul and death. Blood was considered to be the seat or life of the soul and was revered with sacred awe. It belonged to God. Together with the soul, blood constituted the being that was created 'in the image and likeness of God.' Atonement could only be made by blood and the sin of the person who had died was expiated through the decay of the blood after death. In the case of someone losing blood at the time of death there was no ritual cleansing and purification of the body in an effort to retain as much blood as possible for atonement. In an additional effort to preserve whatever blood was remaining, aloes (a bitter aromatic) and myrrh (a resin) were used to anoint the unwashed body. Jewish tradition also insisted that the unpleasant sight of a human face disfigured at the time of death should be concealed.

What the Spanish team has shown is that the Sudarium was used to cover the head of a male who was already dead. They've established that he died in an upright position with his arms outstretched and his head tilted 20% to the right, 70% forward. Crucifixion was the cause of death. The victim died of asphyxiation which results in pulmonary oedema, a mixture of blood and water in the ratio of 5 to 1, collecting in the lungs. He remained in the upright position described for approximately 45 minutes after death. If a body is moved or jolted after death this oedema then surges through the nostrils.

The Sudarium shows evidence of a hand over the cloth clasping the nostrils of the deceased to staunch the flow of this post mortem pleural oedema. This action, in conformity with Jewish concepts of the value of blood as the only currency for atonement, was an effort to staunch the flow of pleural oedema and retain as much blood as possible within the corpse. These form the main stains on the sudarium.

Death by crucifixion was so cruel and painful and also so degrading that, by official imperial decree, no Roman citizen was ever condemned to die in this obscene manner. Most victims were left on their crosses to rot or be eaten by vultures. But Jewish custom insisted on burial. To remain unburied was a solemn dishonour, even repulsive to the Jews, and this is why efforts were made to bury Jesus as quickly as possible.

By analysing post mortem blood (blood which seeped from the corpse after death) and vital blood, (blood which flowed while the victim was still alive) the team showed the time frame of events evident on the Sudarium as concurrent with Good Friday on Calvary. They determined that from the time of death to that of burial approximately 2 hours elapsed. The Sudarium was folded to cover the head of the crucified victim whilst still on the cross. It was then removed and re-wrapped and tied in a knot over the head after the body was lowered and the obstruction created by the position of the arm removed. Remember that while nailed to the cross the head lay angled towards the chest and arm on the cross. The body was then laid horizontally on the ground for 45 minutes resting on the side of its face. Finally it was moved and the Sudarium removed from the head.

Mark Guscin explained all this and a lot more when I filmed his demonstration of how the Sudarium was used and how the stains were formed. He explained that in spite of the Sudarium being a worthy subject of investigation in and of itself, it becomes even more significant when compared with the Shroud of Turin. Both contain human blood, type AB. Both show notable similarity, virtually exact in size and position, of stains from vital blood caused by puncture wounds at the base of the neck, puncture wounds caused by thorns.

When Dr Alan Whanger applied the polarized image overlay technique to the Sudarium comparing it with the blood stains of the shroud it revealed 70 points of coincidence on the front and 50 points on the back. The nose is exactly the same length, swollen and displaced to the right in both cloths. Anthropologically the dimensions of the facial features conclude that both cloths covered the same victim, a man who was beaten and crucified, but also a man who had been crowned with thorns.

Now there were thousands of crucifixions during the Roman occupation of Palestine but none we know of that was simultaneously crowned with thorns. And none that had people so devoted to the victim's memory that they were committed to preserving for posterity two worthless pieces of bloody cloth. Cries of fakery are weak when one understands that by the time the medieval fascination with relics was at fever pitch the Sudarium had already been in Spain for six hundred years. If some one had decided to falsify a cloth such as the Sudarium then why would they bother to make sure it had human blood on it? Why not just use animal blood? Nobody in the middle ages knew the difference. How would they get two cloths to align in so many microscopic details? How would a medieval fraudster know that science would one day be able to reveal the secrets of blood type, or pollen, or dust, or pigment, or textiles? Why would they ensure it conformed to the ratio of pulmonary oedema resultant from crucifixion? The enigma deepens when revelations regarding the Sudarium conform so precisely to the Shroud and to Biblical accounts of the suffering, death, burial and resurrection of Jesus of Nazareth.

Following the trail of relics related to the blood of Christ led us to a third source. This was in the 'Venice of the North', a place of canals and medieval architecture, the enchanting showpiece of the Belgian tourist industry, the city of Bruge. Not many of the thousands of visitors to Bruge would know that it houses one of the most important treasures of the Church: a vial of blood taken as it dripped from the man who was nailed to the cross on Calvary. Gruesome as it may seem, tradition has it that it was collected by Joseph of Arimathea, the high placed Sadducee and member of the Sanhedrin whose status and influence saw to it that the corpse of Jesus was allowed to be removed from the cross by himself and others. Jesus was then laid in the rock-hewn tomb that he, Joseph, had earmarked for his own future burial. The story goes that the vial found its way from Jerusalem to Bruge when the Count of Flanders returned from the Second Crusade. The vial has never been opened let alone scientifically tested yet it has been continuously venerated by the city for over 800 years. To this day this relic is celebrated in an annual grand procession.

My camera explored it from every angle and in extreme close-up but we could probe no deeper. In this instance our curiosity took us no further than that granted every tourist and pilgrim. Our hope is that the blood in this vial may too be the subject of laboratory tests and genetic analysis and so become yet another piece in the puzzle of what might be the connection between God and what remains of His physical incarnation.

Science itself fuels our hopes and anticipation with its promise of rapid development in this our current age of bio-technology. Contemporary forensic analysis together with sophisticated computer modelling is becoming more and more competent to extract data from ancient and degraded sources of blood. It is anticipated that in the very near future advancements in technology will enable DNA identification of samples of degraded blood. From our research this profiling is a distinct possibility if not a probability. If blood samples from the Argentine eucharistic miracle, the Lanciano eucharistic miracle, the Oviedo cloth, the vial of blood in Bruge, the blood from the Bolivian statue and the blood on the two cloths were all submitted to advanced processes of blood analysis for genetic information, the results may well reveal that there is indeed a laboratory test for Christness.

If the samples reveal a common genetic profile then what will they say of his paternity, considering the Church's belief in the Virgin birth? Will there be revelations of his divinity? This blood, which for millions of believers is the price paid for their redemption, may well hold secrets much like those dormant in the shroud and the tilma until technology was invented which unlocked their photographic and chemical properties. Analysis has made them even more mysterious, and more venerable than before. Concurrence of identity revealed by blood analysis of a variety of sources would certainly have an enormous impact.

I remembered what Dr Robert Lawrence said to Mike Willesee and me after it was revealed to him that the human blood and delicate skin he identified microscopically had miraculously formed on a cheap plaster statue:

"My father was a pure scientist, a nuclear physicist, a Nobel prizewinner. He invented the cyclotron which split the atom and more or less started the nuclear age that we're all experiencing today. He died in the 1950's. I wish we had him here right now. I'm sure he'd be very interested in something like this. Give me some good advice. I think it would be wonderful if one single supernatural or miracle type event were to be actually proven. Spectacular. I think it would be of great benefit to mankind. It would make us scientists sit on our hind legs. Make us do some re-thinking." He then smiled broadly, "On the other hand I would feel gratification in showing that this is a fraud."

We are living in an age of bio-technology, one of the most exciting periods of scientific exploration. We are able to see and examine the very building blocks of life. What will this ability pronounce when directed to examine the one who is believed to be the author of life itself? Is the blood on the Shroud and the Sudarium concealing a truth patiently awaiting the time when technology is able to expose it?

(1)   Wilson and Schworz *The Turin Shroud*
         Michael O'Mara Books, London, 2000
(2)   ibid
(3)   ibid

CHAPTER 22

FAITH OF
MY FATHERS

Between the toe of Italy and Sicily lie the Aeolian islands. It is these small Mediterranean islands with their centuries of history and culture that my family left behind for the unknown in Australia. In the cemeteries beside the beautiful and historic churches lie the remains of my great-grandparents, and their parents and grandparents too. The tombstone of my great-grandfather records the usual accolades, that he was a good man and father, and an additional and rather unusual testament to his being a fierce and dedicated son of the Catholic faith of his country. It dawned on me that what my grand parents did not leave behind when they left the islands was their faith. And specifically a continuous devotion to the Rosary, a devotion which accompanied my mother to her death. My old uncle told me of how the church bells would ring on the islands every afternoon at 4.00pm. Everyone would be summoned to pray the Rosary. Why 4.00pm? Why the Rosary?

The answer lay inside some of the ancient churches on the Sicilian mainland, in paintings which honour a triumphant Virgin Mary holding a rosary, below whom is depicted a chaotic naval battle. In the churches on the islands are the same though less detailed depictions. I asked what was going on. The answer was always the same: Lepanto.

The Battle of Lepanto, I learned, was a mighty clash between the navies of the Ottoman Empire and European Christendom on

7 October 1571. Historians have called it the most decisive naval battle anywhere on the globe since the Battle of Actium in 31 BC. It was certainly one of the biggest and bloodiest.

For some years Pope Pius V had been calling for a curtailment to the steady invasion of the Muslim Ottoman Empire into Europe. After 900 years of expansion they virtually ruled the Mediterranean. Malta had been attacked and in 1570 so was Cyprus. Vienna had been a repeated target and even besieged. Theirs was more than simple commercial conquest. The Holy Father was calling for more than protection of livelihood and nations. The whole of Christendom, he warned, was at stake. In response hundreds of great warships and a motley collection of vessels from a coalition of European states rallied to the Pope's call. Spanish, Venetian, Genoese, Portuguese and Papal ships all came together under the command of Don Juan, the 25 year old illegitimate son of the Austrian monarch.

The Pope not only called for action. He called for prayer. He sent out an urgent call to every man, woman and child to join him in the favoured prayer of the Virgin Mary, the holy Rosary. Dread and awe surely filled my ancestors watching from their Aeolian shores as this great procession of masts and sails, of hundreds of battleships made its way to the assigned meeting place in the Bay of Messina. They too would have been praying on the cliffs as the awesome spectacle unfolded before their eyes.

The coalition was well aware of the import of the impending conflict. Philip II of Spain prayed for the protection of Our Lady of Guadalupe and presented the flagship of the Spanish contingent with a reproduction of the miraculous image recently sent from his colony across the Atlantic. The Pope sent a copy of the Shroud of Christ, one which had solemnly been laid on the original, to Don Juan the young commander. He wore it as a sash, literally and figuratively girding himself with the risen Christ.[1]

All night long the Pope prayed the Rosary in the Basilica of Santa Maria Maggiore in Rome. From dawn to dusk and throughout the night the people of Europe joined him to storm heaven in supplication. Into the next day the prayers continued.

The two Titans faced each other off the coast of Greece at Lepanto. Over 500 galleons and hundreds of smaller vessels filled the whole bay. It did not look good for the Christian alliance. They were outnumbered both in men and vessels. The wind was very much against them. Also, Don Juan had ordered the removal of the heavy iron rams which in normal circumstances would have been used by his battleships to sink their opponents. But these were not normal circumstances because the Turks had over 18,000 Christian slaves chained to their galleys as oarsmen, men considered as Christian brothers who would have drowned with their sinking ships had they been rammed. The Holy Alliance would not risk sacrificing them even if it severely handicapped their chances of victory.

(1)
I couldn't dismiss the reflection that these two images remain, nearly five hundred years later, as the standards for a new confrontation, this time not between mighty armed forces but between more subtle opponents: belief and non-belief. Who could have predicted that they would be once again in the avant-garde of a new evangelization? My mind was cast back to a quiet Bolivian church where I was fascinated by a painting representing a vision of St John Bosco. It was a prophetic vision in which he saw the Church as a storm-tossed ship being guided through two columns in the middle of the turbulent seas of the future. On top of one column was devotion to the Virgin Mary. On the other side was devotion to the Holy Eucharist.

Mass was celebrated on each ship. Then Don Juan boarded a small swift vessel and sailed down the line of his ships shouting encouragement to each. When he returned to his flagship, from which he would command the battle, the wind had suddenly changed. It was now in his favour. Thousands of coalition oarsmen rowed out to meet the enemy chanting the Ave Maria. The two massive navies engaged in an awesome five hour confrontation of fierce hand-to-hand fighting, with bows and arrows, swords, daggers and canon fire. The blood of almost 35 000 men turned the blue of the sea to red.

Meanwhile the Pope and the people prayed. By late afternoon at 4.00pm of the 7 October, the exhausted Pope rose and went to the window of the basilica of Santa Maria Maggiore. He gazed out and burst into tears. Vatican archival documents tell how he then turned to face the congregation with the exultant words: "The Christian fleet is victorious! Our great task at present is to thank God for the victory he has given."

The victory was decisive and crushing. It marked a turning point in the history of Christianity and of Europe. Between 25,000 and 30,000 Turks and 9,000 Christians lost their lives. 200 of the 270 Muslim vessels were destroyed. There was no way that anyone hundreds of miles away in Rome could have known of the outcome until news reached there by the usual means, a journey of days. There was certainly no way that anyone could have known that the Holy Alliance claimed victory at exactly 4.00pm.[2]

(2)
One of the Christians at Lepanto who was injured, (he lost his left hand), was Miguel de Cervantes. He was later captured by the Muslims and made a slave in Tunis. A religious order, the Trinitarians, paid his ransom and he was released and went on to write one of Spain's greatest literary treasures, 'Don Quixote'

The Pope attributed the victory to the intervention of the Virgin Mary and declared the 7 October as the Feast of Our Lady of the Rosary. The Aeolian Islands had been saved from invasion and in thanksgiving it would seem they continued in the 4 o'clock devotion to the Rosary and the practice of the Catholic faith in the centuries that followed.

What drives that faith is the belief that death is not the end. Only a door. And what lies beyond that door is an eternal paradise, beautiful beyond our limited imagination. Jesus spoke of it to Katya:

When the cross of suffering weighs on you remember that you are no more than pilgrims on this earth. On the other side of the tomb, there is a world marvellously more beautiful, that God has prepared for his faithful children... [3]

Virgin Mary and Rosary statue in Church on Panarea

*Pope Pius V and Don Juan in prayer at Bay of Messina, before battle of Lepanto, 1571
(Church of St Domenic, Palermo)*

But today there are few of us who seriously consider ourselves as pilgrims on this earth and even fewer still who seriously have faith in the promise of a 'world marvelously more beautiful' than we can understand or imagine. We prefer to avoid thinking about death, mostly because many believe it is the absolute end. There is nothing afterwards. The possibility that there is a God who might have prepared a heaven for us doesn't sit comfortably with modern day thinking.

We come away from our schools and universities encouraged to deny a spiritual side to our existence. For them all that exists is what we can measure, see and touch. Their truth is that we evolved from a chance alliance of chemical processes and physical laws after an explosion, a big bang, billions of years ago. That 'chance' event is now considered by leading astronomers and physicists to have involved such incredibly favourable and minutely calibrated conditions that our existence by 'chance' seems to be a mathematical impossibility. And yet still we cling stubbornly to the notion that we are animals evolved by chance without meaning to live and die in a meaningless world. But are we really just accidental freaks of nature or is there a God who created us and the universe we live in?

We depend on the brilliance of modern science to provide us with answers and yet it has shown itself unable to provide any for the phenomena I have related in this book. These cases which I have filmed and documented extensively for years suggest to me that there is another component to be factored into our understanding and appreciation of ourselves and our world. That component is spiritual and it operates in accordance with another set of laws. The story of Fatima; a plaster statue of Christ which weeps tears and sheds blood; a woman who experiences the wounds of the crucifixion; communion hosts that have turned into living flesh; the inexplicable images of the Shroud and the tilma; blind people who are given

Ron's father Antonino, during a visit to Panarea in 1981

Ron's children at the grave of their great, great grandparents, (Panarea 2004)

perfect sight for thirty minutes. All these are contemporary realities and should surely have a place on the agenda for all thinking people.

My own personal exploration of the big questions of life and death and meaning started after the 'Aliprandi' land incident and have been answered beyond my wildest imagination. God is real. God is relevant.

Choosing to deny this or choosing the hope and comfort of a spiritual life, a life seeking to know and follow God and his laws, is one that we will be obliged to consider in our final moments. There is no escape. Jesus spoke of this final day. The final words shall be his.

"Those who have consumed all their lives and have lost sleep, health, and soul in accumulating goods and income, nothing will they take with them after death. The unfortunate will open their eyes and nothing will they see of what they have acquired at the cost of so much effort. Go to a cemetery where the rich and poor are buried and see if you can distinguish between them. They are all naked and do not have anything but a few fleshless bones.

How much help would the memory of death be for those who live in the midst of the world? Let us see, if at the sight of so many corpses they remember that they will die and that one day they will be as these. Maybe they will awaken from the deadly dream in which they find themselves.

Each step that man takes, each time he breathes, he gets closer to death. Where do all the fatigues he has suffered in this world to acquire fame lead? They will be thrown into the tomb that will bury all his pride and vanity.

If man has lived distractedly, given to the business of this world, what will his affliction be when the terror of death starts to take over his soul and forces him to think of the fate that awaits him? Then he will wish for another month, another week, in order to better straighten his accounts and pacify his conscience. He shall seek peace and not find it. He who finds that he has corresponded to the light and inspiration that he received will be rewarded. And the one that did not will be condemned...... Attend then to My things, to My Kingdom and its justice. For I will not stop providing for what you need. You will be saved and will get the treasure of eternal joy that no one can take away from you." [4]

"One day I will judge My chosen ones and the damned. All shall come before me and all of the world from which they shall receive applause

or condemnation according to how they had listened to Me or forgotten Me. The chosen ones, together with Me will applaud those who meditated My Words. But over all, I, the Eternal Word, will give to each one a price in proportion to the welcome they gave me in life. Now I judge only in private. But one day all My judgements shall be made public. Then unknown persons shall be seen to go up to the highest level and very well-known men descend much. All shall be proportionate to the love or lack of love that each one has shown" [5]

"For this, if you love Me, reflect on what I say, without which you cannot love Me in truth. Use the temporal gifts only to preserve life in this brief space of time that you shall live. Meditate without ceasing, that you are just passing by here. But you are in charge of a very important commission, your salvation and the salvation of your brothers" [6]

(3)   Crusade of Salvation (25)
(4)   Crusade of Salvation (81)
(5)   Crusade of Salvation (82)
(6)   Crusade of Salvation (81)

Selections from the messages received by Katya Rivas are interspersed throughout this book. Here, in its entirety, is one of her written works. Unlike others which are entirely dictated this one includes passages of her own personal reflections and expression.

The Testimony of Catalina on the Holy Mass

This is the testimony that I must and want to give to the whole world, for the greater Glory of God and for the salvation of all of those who want to open their hearts to the Lord. It is also given so that many souls consecrated to God will revive the fire of their love for Christ, some of whom are the owners of the hands that have the power to bring Him to our world so that He can become our nourishment. It is also given for others so that they break loose of the 'routine practice' of receiving Him and revive the amazement of this daily encounter with love. And it is given so that my brothers and sisters from the entire world live the greatest miracle with their hearts: the celebration of the Eucharist.

It was the vigil of the Annunciation and the members of our group had gone to Confession (the Sacrament of Reconciliation). Some of the ladies of the prayer group had not been able to go, and so they left their confession for the next day before the Mass.

When I arrived at church the next day, a little bit late, the Archbishop and priests were already coming out of the sacristy. The Virgin Mary said with her soft and feminine voice that sweetens one's soul,

"Today is a day of learning for you and I want you to pay close of attention because of what you will witness today. Everything that you will experience today, you will have to share with all of mankind."

I was surprised without understanding why, but I tried to be very attentive. The first thing I noticed was the distant sound of beautiful choir voices. The music seemed to draw nearer and then recede like the sound of the wind. The Archbishop began Mass and, when he reached the Penitential Rite, the Virgin Mary said,

"Now ask the Lord from the bottom of your heart to forgive you your sins for they are offensive to Him. In this way you will be able to participate worthily in this privilege of assisting at the Holy Mass."

For a fraction of a second I thought "surely I am in a state of grace, I went to confession last night." she answered,

"Do you think that since last night you have not offended the Lord? Let Me remind you of a couple of things. When you left to come here, the girl who helps you approached to ask you for something and as you were late and in a hurry, you did not answer her in a very nice way. There was a lack of charity on your part and you say, you have not offended God...? While on the way here, a bus crossed over your lane and almost hit you. You expressed yourself in a very non-advisable way against that poor man, instead of saying your prayers and preparing yourself for Mass. You have failed in charity and lost your peace and patience. And you say you have not hurt the Lord? You arrive at the last minute when the procession of the celebrants is already coming out to celebrate the Mass... and you are going to participate without previous preparation..."

I answered, "Alright, my Mother, say no more to me. You do not have to remind me of more things because I am going to die of grief and shame."

"Why do you all arrive at the last minute? You should have come earlier to be able to pray and to ask the Lord to send His Holy Spirit. It is He Who grants you a spirit of peace and Who banishes the spirit of the world, your worries, your problems and distractions in order to enable you to live this so sacred moment. However, you arrive when the celebration is about to commence and you participate as if it is an ordinary event, without any spiritual preparation. Why? This is the greatest of all miracles.. You are going to experience the greatest gift of God from on High and you do not know how to appreciate it."

This was enough. I felt so bad that I had more than enough to ask for forgiveness from God. It was not only for the offenses of that day, but for all the times, like so many other people, that I had waited for the priest to finish his homily before entering the Church. It was also for the times that I did not know or refused to understand what it meant to be there, and for the times that perhaps my soul was full of more serious sins and I had dared to participate in the Holy Mass.

Since this was a Feast day and the Gloria was to be recited. Our Lady said,

"Glorify and bless the Holy Trinity with all your love, in acknowledgement that you are one of Its creatures."

How different was that Gloria! Suddenly I saw myself in a far off place full of light, before the Majestic Presence of the Throne of God. With so much love I went on thanking Him, as I repeated: "For your immense Glory we praise You, we bless You, we adore You, we give You glory, we give You thanks, Lord, God, Heavenly King, God the Father Almighty." And I recalled the paternal face of the Father, full of kindness. "Lord Jesus Christ, only Son of the Father, Lord God, Lamb of God, You take away the sins of the world…" And Jesus was in front of me, with that face full of tenderness and Mercy…"For You alone are the Holy One, You alone are the Lord, You alone are the most High Jesus Christ with the Holy Spirit…", the God of beautiful Love. In that moment my whole being trembled…

And I asked, "Lord, free me from all evil spirits. My heart belongs to You. My Lord, send me Your peace so that I can gain the finest benefits from the Eucharist and that my life produces the best fruits. Holy Spirit of God, transform me, act within me, guide me. Oh God, give me the gifts that I need to serve you better!"

The moment of the Liturgy of the Word arrived and the Virgin made me repeat,

"Lord, today I want to listen to Your Word and produce abundant fruit. May Your Holy Spirit clean the interior of my heart so that Your Word grows and develops in it, purifying my heart so that it may be well disposed."

Our Lady said, *"I want you to be attentive to the readings and to all of the homily of the priest. Remember that the Bible says that the Word of God does not return without bearing fruit. If you are attentive, something from all that you heard will remain in you. You should try to recall all day long those words that left an impression on you. Sometimes it may be two verses, other times the reading of the entire Gospel or maybe only one word. Savour them for the rest of the day and they will then become part of you, because that is the way to change ones life by allowing the Word of God to transform you. And now, tell the Lord that you are here to listen, that you want Him to speak to your heart today."*

Once again I thanked God for giving me the opportunity to hear His Word. And I asked Him for forgiveness for having had such a hard heart for so many years and for having taught my children that they had to go to Mass on Sundays because it is commanded by the Church and not for love and the need to be filled with God. I have attended so many Eucharistic Celebrations mostly out of obligation and, because of this, I believed I was saved. Being alert, not dreaming, paying attention to the readings and the homily of the priest is what I should have been doing!

How much pain I felt for so many years of needless loss because of my ignorance! How superficial is our attendance at the Mass when we go only because someone is getting married or for a funeral Mass or because we have to be seen by society! How much ignorance about our Church and the Sacraments! How much waste in trying to instruct and enlighten ourselves about the things of the world, which in a moment can disappear leaving us with nothing and, at the end of our life, not serve to extend a minute to our existence! However, we know nothing of that which will give us a little of heaven in this world and, afterwards, eternal life. And we call ourselves cultured men and women!

A moment later it was the Offertory and the Holy Virgin said,

"Pray like this: (and I repeated after her) **Lord, I offer all that I am, all that I have, all that I can. I put everything into Your Hands. Build it up, Lord, with the little thing that I am. By the merits of Your Son, transform me, God Almighty. I petition You for my family, for my benefactors, for each member of our Apostolate, for all the people who fight us, for those who commend themselves to my poor prayers. Teach me to lay down my heart on the ground so that their walk may be less hard. This is how the saints prayed; this is how I want you to do it."**

Thus, this is how Jesus asks us to pray, that we put our hearts on the ground so that they do not feel the hardness, but rather that we alleviate the pain of their steps. Years later, I read a book of prayers of a Saint whom I loved dearly, Josemaria Escriva de Balaguer, and in that book I found a prayer similar to that which the Virgin taught me. Perhaps this Saint, to whom I entrust myself, pleased the Virgin with those prayers.

Suddenly some figures whom I had not seen before began to stand up. It was as if from the side of each person present in the Cathedral, another person emerged and soon the Cathedral became full of young, beautiful people. They were dressed in very white robes and they were moving into the central aisle heading towards the Altar. Our Mother said,

"Observe. They are the Guardian Angels of each one of the persons who are here. This is the moment in which your guardian angel carries your offerings and petitions before the Altar of the Lord."

At that moment, I was completely astonished, because these beings had such beautiful faces, so radiant one could not imagine. Their countenance was very beautiful, with almost feminine faces; however, the structure of their body, their hands, their height was masculine. Their naked feet did not touch the floor, but rather they went as if gliding. That procession was very beautiful. Some of them had like a golden plate with something that shone a great deal with a golden-white light. The Virgin said;

"They are the Guardian Angels of the people who are offering this

Holy Mass for many intentions, those people who are conscious of what this celebration signifies, those who, have something to offer the Lord. Offer at this moment... offer your sorrows, your pains, your hopes, your sadness, your joys, your petitions. Remember that the Mass has infinite value. Therefore, be generous in offering and in asking."

Behind the first group of Angels came others who had nothing in their hands; they were coming empty handed. The Virgin said,

"Those are the angels of the people who are here but never offer anything. They have no interest in living each liturgical moment of the Mass and they have no gifts to carry before the Altar of the Lord."

At the end of the procession came other angels who were rather sad, with their hands joined in prayer but with their eyes downcast.

"These are the Guardian Angels of the people who are here but do not want to be, that is to say of the people who have been forced to come here, who have come out of obligation but without any desire to participate in the Holy Mass. The angels go forth sadly because they have nothing to carry to the Altar, except for their own prayers.

Do not sadden your Guardian Angel. Ask for much, ask for the conversion of sinners, for peace in the world, for your families, your neighbors, for those who ask for your prayers. Ask, ask for much, not only for yourselves, but for others as well.

Remember the offering that most pleases the Lord is the one in which you offer yourselves as a holocaust so that upon his descent Jesus may transform you by His own merits. What do we have to offer the Father on our own? Nothing but sin. But the offering of ourselves united to the merits of Jesus, that offering is pleasing to the Father."

That sight, that procession was so beautiful that it would be difficult to compare it to another. All those celestial creatures being reverent before the Altar, some leaving their gifts on the floor, others prostrating themselves on their knees with their foreheads almost touching the floor. As soon as they arrived at the altar they disappeared from my sight.

At the end of the Preface and when the assembly said, "Holy, Holy, Holy", suddenly everything that was behind the celebrants disappeared. Behind the left side of the Archbishop thousands of Angels appeared in a diagonal line: small angels, big angels, angels with immense wings, angels with small wings, angels without wings. Like the others, all were dressed with tunics like the white robes of the priests or altar boys.

Everyone knelt with their hands joined in prayer and in reverence, bowing their heads. Beautiful music was heard as if there were many choirs with different voices, all singing in unison together with the people: "Holy, Holy, Holy…"
The moment of the Consecration, that moment of the most marvellous of miracles had arrived. Another great multitude appeared in a diagonal line behind the Bishop, this time to his right. They were similarly dressed, but in various shades of pastel colors: rose, green, light blue, lilac, yellow, in short, in different and very soft colors. Their faces were also brilliant, full of joy. They all seemed to be the same age. You could notice, I can't say why that they were people of different ages but their faces looked the same, without wrinkles, happy. They too knelt down at the singing of "Holy, Holy, Holy Lord…"

Our Lady said,
"These are the Saints and the Blessed of Heaven and among them are the souls of your relatives who already enjoy the Presence of God."

Then I saw Her, exactly to the right of the Archbishop, a step behind the celebrant. She was suspended a little off the floor, kneeling on some very fine, transparent but at the same time luminous fabric, like crystalline water, the Holy Virgin, with hands joined, looking attentively and respectfully at the celebrant. She spoke to me from there, but silently, directly to the heart, without looking at me.

"Truly, does it surprise you to see me standing a little behind the Archbishop? This is how it should be… For all the love that My Son bestows upon me, He has not given me the dignity that He has given the priests of being able to perform the daily Miracle with my hands as they do with their priestly hands. Because of this, I feel a deep respect for priests and for the miracle that God carries out through them, which compels me to kneel here behind them."

My God, how much dignity, how much grace the Lord pours over the priestly souls and neither we, nor even some of them, are conscious of this.

Before the Altar, grey shadows of people appeared with their hands raised. The Holy Virgin said,

"These are the blessed souls of Purgatory, who await your prayers in order to be refreshed. Do not stop praying for them. They pray for you but they cannot pray for themselves. It is you who have to pray for them, to help them leave Purgatory to be with God and to enjoy Him eternally. You now see it; I am here all the time. People go on pilgrimages, searching for the places where I have appeared. This is good because of all the graces that they will receive there. But in no apparition, in no other place, am I more present than in the Holy Mass. At the foot of the Altar where the Eucharist is celebrated, you will always find Me; in front of the Tabernacle I remain with the angels because I am always with Him."

To see our Blessed Mother's beautiful face at that moment of the "Holy" as well as everyone else with their radiant faces, with hands joined waiting for that miracle which is repeated continuously. It was like being in Heaven itself. And to think that at that moment there are people who can be distracted in conversation. It hurts me to tell you, many men, more than women, stand with their arms crossed, as if paying homage to the Lord as one equal to another.

The Virgin said,
"Tell men that they are never more manly than when they bend their knees before God."

The celebrant said the words of the Consecration. Though he was a person of normal height he suddenly began to grow in stature, becoming filled with light, a supernatural golden-white light, which surrounded him and grew very strong around the face. This happened in such a way that I could not see his features. As he raised the Host, I saw his hands and on the back of his hands he had marks from which emanated a great deal of light. It was Jesus! It was He Who wrapped His Body around the celebrant, as He lovingly surrounded the hands of the Archbishop. At that moment the Host began to grow and become enormous and upon it the marvellous face of Jesus appeared. He looked down upon His people. Instinctively I wanted to bow my head and Our Lady said,

"Do not look down. Look up to view and contemplate Him. Exchange your gaze with His and repeat the prayer of Fatima: Lord, I believe, I adore, I trust and I love You. I ask You to pardon all those who do not believe, do not adore, do not trust and do not love You. Forgiveness and Mercy… Now tell Him how much you love Him and pay your homage to the King of Kings."

I said the prayer and it seemed as if I was the only one He was looking at from the enormous Host. But I knew that this was the way He gazed at each person, with boundless love .. Then I lowered my head until I had my forehead on the floor, as did all the Angels and the blessed from Heaven. Perhaps for a fraction of a second, I thought that it was Jesus Who then took on the body of the celebrant and at the same time He was inside the Host. As he lowered the Host, the celebrant returned to his normal size. Tears ran down my cheeks; I was unable to recover from my astonishment. As the Archbishop said the words of the Consecration of the wine, lightning appeared from the heavens and in the background. The walls and ceiling of the church disappeared. All was dark except that brilliant light from the Altar.

Suddenly, suspended in the air I saw the crucified Jesus from His head to the lower part of His chest. The horizontal beam of the Cross was sustained by large, strong hands. Amid this splendour, a light resembling a very brilliant, very small dove, appeared and flew swiftly all over the Church. It came to rest on the left shoulder of the Archbishop, who continued to appear as Jesus because I could distinguish His long hair, His luminous wounds and His large body, but I could not see His face.

Above was Jesus crucified, His head fallen upon His right shoulder. I was able to contemplate His face, beaten arms and torn flesh. On the right side of His chest He had an injury and it started to ooze. Toward the left side blood flowed out and on the right side I think flowed very brilliant water. It was more like light gushing and moving from right to left, being directed toward the faithful. The amount of blood that flowed out toward the Chalice amazed me. I thought it would overflow and stain everything on the Altar, but there was not a single drop spilled. At that moment the Virgin said:

"This is the miracle of miracles. I repeat to you that the Lord does not exist in time or space. At the moment of the Consecration, all the assembly is brought to the foot of Calvary, at the instant of the crucifixion of Jesus."

Can anyone imagine that? Our eyes cannot see it, but we are there at the very moment that they are crucifying Jesus. He is asking for forgiveness to the Father, not only for those who put Him to death, but also for each one of our sins: **"Father forgive them because they know not what they do."**

Ever since that day, I do not care if the world thinks I am crazy, but I ask everybody to kneel and try to live, with their heart and with all their sensibility that they are capable of, this privilege that the Lord grants us.

As we were about to pray the Our Father, *the Lord spoke for the first time during the celebration and said:*

"Wait, I want you to pray from the deepest recesses of your being. At this moment, bring to mind that person or persons who have done you the greatest harm during your life, so that you can hold them close to your chest and tell them with all your heart: 'In the Name of Jesus I forgive you and wish you peace. In the Name of Jesus, I ask for your forgiveness and wish my peace.' If the person is worthy of that peace, then the person will receive it and feel better for it. If that person is not capable of opening up to that peace, then peace will return to your heart. But I do not want you to receive nor offer peace when you are not capable of forgiving and feeling that peace in your heart first. Be careful of what you do, when you repeat in the Our Father: 'forgive us our trespasses as we forgive those who trespass against us'. If you are capable of forgiving but not forgetting, as the saying goes, you are placing conditions upon the forgiveness of God. You are saying: You forgive me only as I am capable of forgiving but no more."

I do not know how to explain my pain, at the realization of how much we can hurt the Lord. And also how much we can injure ourselves by having so many grudges, bad feelings and unflattering things that are born from our own prejudices and feelings. I forgave; I forgave from the heart and asked for forgiveness from all the people whom I had hurt at one time or another, in order to feel the peace of the Lord.

The celebrant said, "...grant us peace and unity..." and, then, "the peace of the Lord be with all of you."

Suddenly I saw among some of the people who were embracing each other, a very intense light between them. I knew it was Jesus and I practically threw myself to embrace the person next to me. I could truly feel the embrace of the Lord in that light. It was He Who embraced me giving me His peace, because in that moment I had been able to forgive and remove from my heart all rancour against others. That is what Jesus wants, to share that moment of joy, embracing each other for we desire His Peace.

The moment of the celebrant's communion arrived. There I once again noticed the presence of all the priests next to the Archbishop. When he took Communion, the Virgin said,

"This is the moment to pray for the celebrant and the priests who accompany him. Repeat together with me: Lord, bless them, sanctify them, help them, purify them, love them, take care of them and support them with Your Love. Remember all the priests of the world, pray for all the consecrated souls..."

Dear brothers and sisters, that is the moment in which we should pray for them, because they are the Church as we, the laity, are also. Many times we, the laity, demand so much from the priests, but we are unable to pray for them, to understand that they are human and to comprehend and appreciate the solitude that many times can surround a priest.

We should understand that the priests are people like ourselves and that they need to be understood, to be cared for. They need affection and attention from us because they are giving their life to each one of us, as Jesus did, being consecrated to Him.

The Lord wants the people of the flock that God has entrusted to him to pray and help in the sanctification of their Pastor. Someday, when we are on the other side, we will understand the marvels that the Lord has done, giving us priests who help us to save our souls.

The people stood up from their pews to receive Communion. The great moment of the encounter had come. The Lord said to me, **"Wait a moment; I want you to observe something..."** An interior impulse made me raise my eyes towards the person who was going to receive Communion on the tongue from the hands of the priest. I should clarify that this person was one of the ladies from our group who the previous night was unable to go to confession but this morning was able to do so before the Holy Mass. When the Priest placed the Sacred Host on her tongue, a flash of light, like a very golden white light, went right through this person, first through her back, then surrounding her from the back, around the shoulders and then the head. The Lord said,

"This is how I Myself rejoice in embracing a soul who comes with a clean heart to receive Me."

The tone of voice of Jesus was that of a happy person. I was amazed to see my friend return to her pew surrounded by light, embraced by the Lord. I thought of the marvel that we miss so many times by going to receive Jesus with our small or large offenses when it should be a feast.

Many times we say that there are no priests to whom to go to confess at any given moment. But the problem is not about confessing at each moment but the problem resides in our ease of falling into evil again. On the other hand, in the same way that we make an effort to search for a beauty parlour or men search for a barber when we have a party, we have to also make an effort to seek a priest when we need to remove all that dirt from ourselves. We must not have the audacity to receive Jesus at any moment with our hearts full of ugliness..
When I went to receive communion, Jesus told me,

"The Last Supper was the moment of the greatest intimacy with My own. During that hour of love, I established what could be thought of as the greatest of lunacy in the eyes of men, that of making Myself a prisoner of Love. I established the Eucharist. I wanted to remain with you until the end of the centuries because My Love could not bear that you become orphans, you whom I loved more than My life."

I received that Host which had a different flavour. It was a mixture of blood and incense that inundated me entirely. I felt so much love that the tears flowed down my cheeks without me being able to stop them.

When I returned to my seat, while kneeling down, the Lord said: *"Listen..."* A moment later I began to hear the prayers of the lady who was seated in front of me and who had just received communion.

What she said without opening her mouth was more or less like this: "Lord, remember that we are at the end of the month and I do not have the money to pay the rent, the car payments or the children's school fees. You have to do something to help me... Please, make my husband stop drinking so much. I cannot bear his being intoxicated any more and my youngest son is going to repeat the year again if you do not help him. He has exams this week... And do not forget our neighbour who is moving. Let her do it right away. I cannot stand her anymore... etc., etc."

Then the Bishop said, "Let us pray," and obviously all the congregation stood up for the final prayer. Jesus said in a sad tone,

"Did you notice the prayer? Not a single time did she tell Me that she loves Me. Not a single time did she thank Me for the gift that I have given her by bringing down My Divinity to her poor humanity, to elevate her to Me. Not a single time has she said: thank You, Lord. It has been a litany of orders... and are just like all of those who come to receive Me. I have died for love and I am resurrected. For love I await each one of you and for love I remain with you... But you do not realize that I need your love. Remember that I am the Beggar of Love in this sublime hour for the soul."

Do you all realize that He, the Love, is begging for our love and we do not give it to Him? Moreover, we avoid going to that encounter with the Love of Loves, with the only love who gives of itself in permanent oblation.

When the celebrant was going to give the blessing, the Holy Virgin said,

"Be attentive, take care... You do any old sign instead of the Sign of the Cross. Remember that this blessing could be the last one that you will receive from the hands of a priest. You do not know when leaving here if you will die or not. You do not know if you will have the opportunity to receive a blessing from another priest. Those consecrated hands are giving you the blessing in the Name of the Holy Trinity. Therefore, make the Sign of the Cross with respect, as if it was the last one of your life."

How much we miss in not understanding and not participating everyday at the Holy Mass! Why not make an effort to begin the day a half hour earlier and run to the Holy Mass and receive all the blessings that the Lord wants to pour over us? I am aware that because of their obligations not everybody can attend daily Mass, but at least two or three times a week. So many avoid Mass on Sundays with the smallest excuse that they have a child, or two, or ten, and, therefore, they cannot attend Mass. How do people manage when they have other important types of commitments? They take all the children or take turns and the husband goes at one hour and the wife another, but they carry out their duty to God.

We have time to study, to work, to entertain, to rest, but WE DO NOT HAVE TIME AT LEAST ON SUNDAY TO GO TO THE HOLY MASS.

Jesus asked me to remain with Him a few minutes more after Mass had finished. He said,

"Do not leave in a hurry after Mass has finished. Stay a moment in My company and enjoy it and let Me enjoy yours…"

As a child I had heard someone say that the Lord remained with us for five or ten minutes, after communion. I asked Him at this moment, "Lord, truly, how much time do You stay with us after communion?" I suppose that the Lord must have laughed at my silliness because He answered,

"All the time that you want to have Me with you. If you speak to Me all day long, offering Me some words during your chores, I will listen to you. I am always with you. It is you who leaves Me. You leave the Mass and the day of obligation ends. You kept the day of the Lord and it is now finished for you. You do not think that I would like to share your family life with you, at least that day. In your homes you have a place for everything and a room for each activity: a room to sleep, another to cook, another to eat, etc. Which place have you made for Me? It should not be a place where you only have an image, which gets dusty all the time, but a place where at least five minutes a day the family meets to give thanks for the day and for the gift of life, to ask for their daily needs, to ask for blessings, protection, health. Everything has a place in your homes, except Me.

Men plan their day, their week, their semester, their vacations, etc. They know what day they are going to rest, what day they will go to the movies or to a party, or visit grandmother or the grandchildren,

the children, their friends and to their amusements. How many families say at least once a month, 'This is the day for our turn to go and visit Jesus in the Tabernacle.' Then the whole family comes to talk to Me. They sit down and talk to Me, telling Me how it has been since the last time, telling Me their problems, the difficulties they have, asking Me about what they need... making Me part of these things! How many times?
I know everything. I read even the deepest secrets of your hearts and minds. But I like that you tell Me about your life and that you enable Me to participate as a family member, as the most intimate friend. How many graces does man lose by not giving Me a place in his life!"

When I remained with Him that day and on many other days, He continued to give us teachings. Today I want to share with you this mission that He has entrusted to me. Jesus said,

"I wanted to save My creature because the moment of opening the door to Heaven has been filled with too much pain... Remember that not even one mother has fed her child with her own flesh. I have gone to that extreme of Love to communicate My merits.
The Holy Mass is Myself prolonging My life and My sacrifice on the Cross among you. Without the merits of My life and My Blood, what do you have to present to the Father? Nothing, misery and sin...
You should exceed in virtue the angels and archangels, because they do not have the joy of receiving Me as nourishment like you do. They drink a drop from the spring, but you that have the grace of receiving Me. You have the whole ocean to drink."

The other thing that the Lord spoke about with pain concerned the people who make a habit out of their encounter with Him, of those who have lost the awe of each encounter with Him. That routine turns some people so lukewarm that they have nothing new to tell Jesus when they receive Him. He also said that there was no small number of consecrated souls who lose their enthusiasm of falling in love with the Lord, and make of their vocation an occupation, a profession to which nothing more is given, except that which is demanded of one, but without feeling...

Then the Lord spoke to me about the fruits that must come from each communion that we receive. It does happen that there are people who receive the Lord daily but do not change their lives. They spend many hours in prayer and do many works, etc. but their life does not go on transforming and a life that does not transform cannot bear true fruits for the Lord. The merits we receive in the Eucharist should bear the fruits of conversion in us and fruits of charity toward our brothers and sisters.

The laity has a very important role in our Church. We do not have the right to be silent in the face of the Lord sending us out, as all the baptized, to go forth and announce the Good News. We do not have the right to absorb all this knowledge and not share it with others and to allow our brothers to die of hunger when we have so much bread in our hands.

We cannot see what may be destroying our Church because we are comfortable in our parishes and homes, receiving so much from the Lord: His Word, the homilies of the priests, the pilgrimages, the Mercy of God in the Sacrament of Reconciliation, the marvellous union with the nourishment of communion, the talks of preachers. In other words, we are receiving so much and we do not have the courage to leave our comfort zone and go to a jail, to a correctional institution, to speak to the neediest. To go and tell them not to give up, that they were born Catholic and that their Church needs them there, suffering, because this suffering will serve to redeem others, because that sacrifice will gain for them eternal life.

We are not capable of going where the terminally ill are in the hospitals and praying the Chaplet of Divine Mercy, to help them with our prayers during that time of struggle between good and evil, to free them from the traps and temptations of the devil. Every dying person has fear and just taking their hand and talking to them about the love of God and the marvel that awaits them in Heaven next to Jesus and Mary, next to their departed ones, gives them comfort.

The times in which we currently live do not permit flirtation with indifference. We must be an extension of the hands of our priests, to go where they cannot reach. But for this, we need courage. We must receive Jesus, live with Jesus, nourish ourselves with Jesus. We are afraid to commit ourselves a little more and when the Lord says, *"First seek the Kingdom of God and the rest will be given to you in addition,"* He says it all, brothers and sisters. It is in the seeking of the Kingdom of God, by all possible means and with all means and... open your hands to receive

EVERYTHING in addition! This is because He is the Master Who pays the best, the only One Who is attentive to your smallest needs.

Brothers and sisters, thank you for allowing me to carry out the mission that was entrusted to me of being able to give you these pages…
The next time you attend the Holy Mass, live it. I know the Lord will fulfill for you His promise that **"The Mass will never be the same for you."** And when you receive Him, love Him! Experience the sweetness of feeling yourself resting along His side, which was pierced for you to leave you His Church and His Mother to open the doors to the House of the Father. Experience this so that you are able to verify His Merciful Love through this testimony and try to communicate with Him with your childlike love.

May God bless you during this Passover of the Resurrection.

Your sister in the Living Jesus,

Catalina (Katya Rivas)

ACKNOWLEDGMENTS

I wish to express my special thanks to Lee Han for the
considerable assistance she gave me in writing this book.
Her great gifts as a writer, researcher and communicator have truly
helped shape this book into something far better than I could ever
have done on my own.

To my wife Gabrielle, my loyal supporter, for her role as my
assistant, researcher and general hand on the numerous fact
finding and filming expeditions overseas in the last 15 years.

My thanks also goes to my personal assistant of many years,
Lyn Petrie, and to Bill Steller, Mike Willesee, Dr Ricardo
Castanõn, Katya Rivas, Father Renzo Sessolo, Father William
Aliprandi, Padre Alejandro Pezet, Padre Eudardo Graham.

To the many professionals I have consulted, including Professor
Angelo Fiori, Professor Odoardo Linoli, Dr. John Walker,
Dr Robert Lawrence, Dr Frederick Zugibe, the late Dr Tom Loy,
Dr Peter Ellis, Dr Colin Summerhays and Dr. Richard Haskell,
I express my appreciation.

Share this book with a friend!

For Additional Copies

Visit Web Sites:

**In the United States
and North America**
www.loveandmercy.org

**Australia and Other
Countries**
www.reasontobelieve.com.au

To obtain the documentary *"A Plea to Humanity"* on DVD produced by the author on Katya Rivas or the documentary referred to in this book, *"The Eucharist - In Communion with Me"* on DVD, visit these web sites:

**In the United States
and North America**
www.loveandmercy.org

**Australia and Other
Countries**
www.apleatohumanity.com

Or Write:

**In the United States
and North America**
Love & Mercy Publications
P. O. Box 1160
Hampstead, NC 28443
USA
www.loveandmercy.org

**Australia and Other
Countries**
Mary Mackillop Bookshop
39 Avoca Drive
Kincumber NSW 2251
Australia
Phone: (+61-2) 4369 5069
Fax: (+61-2) 4382 3300